Jack Wilson: Glacier pilot, Big Game Outfitter, Guide, Author.

Jack Wilson is a living legend. From WWII combat missions, to daring rescue flights on the highest peaks in North America, to guiding for majestic Dall sheep, Jack has led a life that most of us can only dream of. His vast experience along with his unique view of Alaska enables him to record an accurate history of Alaska in a captivating style. Although Jack is known as a premier pilot in Alaska's short history, his books indicate his true calling may be that of Author.

DEDICATION

To my wife, Bonnie, and my sons, T.J. and Tony.

THE QUEST FOR DALL SHEEP

A HISTORIC GUIDE'S MEMORIES
OF ALASKAN HUNTING

BY JACK WILSON

NORTHERN PUBLISHING — WASILLA, ALASKA

THE QUEST FOR DALL SHEEP:
A Historic Guide's Memories of Alaskan Hunting
by Jack Wilson

Editor: Tony Russ

Published by: **Northern Publishing**
574 Sarahs Way
Wasilla, AK 99654

All rights reserved. No part of this book may be reproduced or transmitted in any form or by any means, electronic or mechanical, including photocopying, recording or by any information storage and retrieval system without written permission from the Publisher, except for the inclusion of brief quotations in a review.

Copyright © 1997 by Jack Wilson
First Printing 1997
Second Printing 2000

Library of Congress Cataloging in Publication Data

ISBN 0-9639869-2-9 $19.95 Softcover

Printed in Alaska

FRONT AND BACK COVER PHOTO: Photo taken in 1961 by Jack Wilson© of Harry L. Swank Jr., holding the World Record Dall sheep horns (still #1 as of November, 1997).

TABLE OF CONTENTS

ACKNOWLEDGEMENTS...		6
FOREWARD..		7
CHAPTER 1	THE QUEST..	9
CHAPTER 2	LURE OF THE DALL SHEEP......................	17
CHAPTER 3	THE WILD SHEEP OF NORTH AMERICA.....	29
CHAPTER 4	SPOTTING AND LOCATING SHEEP.............	41
CHAPTER 5	BUILDING THE AIRSTRIPS........................	45
CHAPTER 6	THE GRAVITY TESTER...............................	57
CHAPTER 7	NEANDERTHALS......................................	67
CHAPTER 8	THE WORLD RECORD DALL RAM..............	77
CHAPTER 9	HELICOPTERS..	87
CHAPTER 10	OUTLAW GUIDES....................................	95
CHAPTER 11	THE BATTERING RAMS.............................	109
CHAPTER 12	A SHEEP HUNT WITH THE DUKE................	119
CHAPTER 13	GOAT HUNT..	125
CHAPTER 14	THE RAM THAT BATTERED.......................	137
CHAPTER 15	MOOSE AT THEIR BEST............................	147
CHAPTER 16	THE BEAR THAT WON..............................	163
CHAPTER 17	CARIBOU ARE STRANGE BUT MARVELOUS CREATURES.........................	173
CHAPTER 18	FACTS ABOUT SHEEP AND HUNTING.........	187
CHAPTER 19	THE LONG YEARS WENT BY......................	211

ACKNOWLEDGEMENTS

I want to thank these people who were kind enough to help me out and keep me straight with needed information:

Lynn Ellis, Ellis Air Taxi; Glenallen, Alaska

Jerry Lee, Bush Pilot; Copper River Basin, Alaska

Bob Tobey, Alaska Department of Fish and Game; Glenallen, Alaska

Jim Hanna, National Park Ranger; Copper Center, Alaska

Bruce Bartley, Alaska Department of Fish and Game; Anchorage, Alaska

FOREWARD

This is the story of Jack Wilson's dream come true—his life as an Alaskan and adventures as a bush pilot and guide. Jack loved Alaska and all it had to offer—this is plainly evident throughout his writings. His story is made up of many intertwined episodes; each comprising a chapter of this book.

To the envy of many of us, Jack got to experience the early days of Alaska's Statehood, before progress changed it. As a bush pilot, air charter operator, and hunting guide, Jack got a firsthand look at an Alaska we can only read about. His experiences with previously-unhunted game herds cannot be duplicated. And his pioneering of trophy Dall sheep hunting in the Wrangell Mountains—in areas that are now closed to most hunters—is almost unimaginable for today's hunters. This background gives Jack the ability to write honest accounts of incredible adventures that would be suspect from almost anyone else.

Readers will be educated by these stories as well as entertained by them. Jack includes his personal opinions about hunting tactics and current hunting opportunities. Several stories describe wildlife habits that haven't changed over time. And Jack's writing style—although honest and straightforward—is full of humor and wonderful poetic descriptions of the wild Alaska he so loves.

So if you are fascinated with Alaska and its history, a hunter, or just a fan of Alaska's wildlife, sit back and enjoy Jack's story. It will take you to a bygone day; you will be both thrilled and saddened as you live through Alaska's prime; this will be a journey for your soul.

The Chitina River valley with the Chugach Mountains in the background. Many of the largest Dall sheep ever taken have come from this area.

CHAPTER 1
THE QUEST

The side of the mountain we were on sloped up steeply, yet not too steep for a man to climb. The setting was beautiful as such things always were in these mountains; great scenery in every direction with some of the highest mountains within view of our lofty perch. This was in the Wrangell Mountains of Alaska which has some of the very highest mountains, although not the highest of all. In the Alaska Range to the northwest was Mt. McKinley, the highest at over 20,000 feet. In our Wrangell Mountains were at least three that topped 16,000 feet—Sanford, Blackburn and Bona; then Mt. Wrangell at 14,000 feet and so on down to the lower elevations. A mountain paradise—it had always been worthy of the beauty it offered to those who can truly enjoy beautiful settings.

From our mountainside perch, things closer than the great height of the mountains gained our attention. We were on a south slope in the sunlight and our view took in the Chitina River—the largest tributary of the Copper River. Several miles across the river system we could easily see the north slope of the Chugach Mountains. They were too far away to see small objects, but we had a wonderful view of these magnificent mountains—which were not as high as the Wrangells, but offered an equal amount of beauty.

We were sitting for a rest at about the 5,000 foot level, a hunter and I, and we were happy and at peace. Around us were the grasses, lichens, and short-stemmed wildflowers that grow with profusion in the summer months. There were still ground squirrels at this elevation and it was pleasant to watch their antics. On another part of this mountain where there were many great boulders in a basin I knew I could show the hunter some hoary marmots. These are larger animals that like to sit on boulders or mounds of dirt and whistle the sound of alarm, but they were not right here where we were at present. We knew we might see other wildlife such as wolverine—which liked to climb up after squirrels—or we might see one of our numerous grizzly bears, hopefully at a good distance. We also knew we would see some Dall sheep because these beautiful, white, thin-horned sheep occupied this very mountain. That is the main reason we were up there, to hunt these sheep and possibly take a trophy ram.

As the guide and an Alaskan, I was becoming very well-acquainted with this hunter who was from one of the states Outside. It is wise for a guide to become well-acquainted since the primary purpose is for the guide to get the hunter what he wants and cater to his whims as much as possible. There are many types of hunters and it was necessary to find out just what it might be that this hunter truly wanted.

So far it was turning out to be a pleasant acquaintance. This hunter, a man of possibly 50 years of age and in good physical condition, was an amiable, pleasant fellow who was in Alaska partly to get a good trophy ram; yet he was there for other reasons as well. He was the type of man that wanted the wilderness experience and to enjoy things as time went on. He claimed that if he did not see just the kind of ram he wanted, he probably would not shoot anything. He was an experienced sheep hunter who had taken a good ram at a previous time and wanted a better trophy if possible. On these particular mountains it was known that there were some very big rams, so the possibility of his getting a great ram was very good. The only way to find out if there was a better ram in this particular place was to go, observe, and hunt.

He was loaded down with good camera gear, too, and took pictures every time we rested on our way up the mountain. He very much hoped to get pictures of the sheep when we reached them. I was beginning to appreciate this man and his outlook on life. Here was a hunter that was no game hog at all who was enjoying himself to the fullest, even though we had not even seen a sheep yet. He was in no hurry. I believed I had a true sportsman on my hands.

The Nabesna Glacier is just one of the tremendous glaciers that add to the spectacular scenery in the Wrangell Mountains.

I fully realized what a spectacular country I had chosen for the area I would guide in for the great white sheep. It was truly an amazing part of Alaska. Right here within our view were some of the greatest glaciers in the entire country. From our lofty perch we could easily see the great Logan and Chitina Glaciers. The Logan Glacier begins in Canada near Mt. Logan, the highest mountain in Canada at more than 18,000 feet. It flows down into Alaska and there it is joined by the Chitina and other glaciers so that, at the terminus (or end) of the glacier, it is several miles wide—a tremendous thing. We could plainly see Mt. Logan itself, a true giant of a mountain. The Chitina River begins where the terminal moraine ends, unlike most rivers which begin high in the mountains. When you think of a river and its beginning, you can see by maps and through hearsay that it starts high in the mountains as a little brook cascading down over the rocks. As it proceeds downward in its inevitable quest to reach the sea, it is joined by other branches and becomes larger. In time it gains the status of a creek and then is joined by other brooks and creeks until at sometime along its course—no one knows exactly where—it becomes a river. It remains in that status until it either joins a larger river or, being the dominant river itself, finally reaches the sea as—all rivers must do.

But the Chitina begins as a full-blown river all at once. It begins in many different channels as it emerges from the glacier. It is loaded with silt, as all glacial rivers are. The many channels flow on separately and it is known as a braided river for many miles through country which at one time had been covered by the glacier, which had by now receded to the point we could see. Finally it combines into one channel between high bluffs and flows on down to the west and joins the equally large Copper River—which is the dominant one. The Chitina River is a short river, being only some 80 miles in its entire length. Yet it is a very *large* river. At one time, years ago, the lower part of the river had been traveled by stern wheel steamboats, before there was a railroad to the great Kennicott Copper Mines—also in the Wrangell mountains.

Thus, we could see the mountains in Canada, the great glacier, the moraine, the beginning and several miles of the river from just where we were sitting. Then I discovered something else. By moving parallel to the mountain for about 50 yards to the west we could look down on spectacular Barnard Glacier, which flows in from the north.

This is also a great glacier with many side moraines of rock and rubble—a beautiful thing. We had, without thinking about it, climbed to a place where we could see more scenery in one look than anyone could imagine. The hunter took full advantage of this, since he had the proper camera equipment and plenty of film. He got some great pictures that day—I'm sure—although I never did seen any of them.

In time we did arrive where there were sheep in the distance and I took over as guide to get us closer. We did get closer and spotted a group of rams, then headed their way, very carefully. We got within range and I realized we were just where we needed to be for a good shot. After observing the rams closely I decided there were probably one or two animals worthy of this hunter's desire. I told him to go up carefully and have a look over the ridge. Before we had gotten that far he had paused and taken out a 35 mm camera equipped with a telephoto lens—which appeared to be the right equipment for what we were doing.

Dall sheep are one of the most difficult, but striking, animals to photograph.

With his rifle and camera, and I alongside to direct him to the proper rams if need be, we got up there where we could see them; some of them lying down and some up feeding. He laid there looking over the little ridge, then gently eased his camera up and focused it on the sheep. He snapped the shutter, then reloaded the camera and trained it on the sheep again. The sheep did not know of our presence and it was an ideal situation. Some of them were lying down and two or three were standing and feeding. As they moved they offered him new shots, so he continued with his camera.

I used my glasses and determined which was the best ram. I was prepared to whisper which ram was the best and fully expected him to reach for his rifle and get ready to shoot. Yet he did not take the rifle, but kept training the camera. Finally he eased down from the ridge, as I did also to ask what he was going to do.

He grinned at me and said he thought he had some very good pictures. I told him about that good ram and suggested he crawl back up there and take it. But then he said no, he did not think so; and something about them being too beautiful to shoot. He was satisfied with only his pictures. This was amazing to me. I was fully prepared to cape out a ram, field-dress it, cut up the meat, and do all the things necessary for a guide to do.

Yet this hunter decided not to shoot at all! And what a relief that was. I grinned back at him and said if that was what he wanted, we could go on back down to base camp, and we did.

It was very gratifying to have a hunter like that one for once in my life.

THE QUEST   15

While hunting sheep, magnificent views like this are common. This is part of the lure that drives hunters in quest of Dall sheep.

Jack Wilson got plenty of flying experience in difficult situations during World War II. This 1944 photo was taken in Grave, Holland. Jack is delivering a jeep and trailer to British soldiers during operation "Market Garden," while surrounded by the German Army.

CHAPTER 2
LURE OF THE DALL SHEEP

The lure of Alaska brought me to her bosom in the early 1950s. There were several reasons for my move to Alaska, but part of it was the attraction of the very numerous white Dall sheep that inhabited many of the mountainous areas of this great land. I was an avid seeker of the wilderness and the animals that lived in this wilderness. The Dall sheep came to the top of the list after I had first seen them in the Alaska Range. I wanted to observe them at close range, hunt them, and take pictures of them.

For qualifications, I had grown up near the mountains of northwest Colorado. Mule deer and elk were plentiful on and near our small cattle ranch and hunting had been a natural part of my young life. I had become a guide when only a teenager and loved the wilderness and hunting.

A person must have a way to make a living and one thing I could do was fly airplanes. I had done many other things as well, but I loved to fly and was quite good at it. During World War II I had gone through the old Army Air Corps Training School and become a qualified pilot. There had been a lot of flying and other training, then I found myself in aerial combat in the African and European Campaigns. Having survived this, I emerged as an experienced pilot and knew I could use this knowledge to make a living.

Colorado had been all right in many ways. I could fly to get by with a fairly decent income and I could spend some of the time in the high wilderness areas as a hunter and guide. There was something more I wanted, however, and it was hard to define. I just had not been able to firmly establish my roots in Colorado and felt the need for a change. Alaska was a possibility, so I tried it.

After almost two years in Alaska, during which time I had flown as a flight instructor and other flying enterprises, I finally arrived at the very small town of Chitina—hired on as a mountain pilot by Cordova Airlines. This was the place, as it turned out, that I would put down my roots—a place to roost. Although the flying pay on this job was very low for a beginner, at least it was something; and there was a chance for advancement. It held my interest immediately. We had mountains—which I loved—on all sides. The town itself was tucked up into the edge of the Chugach Mountains on the Copper River, opposite the mouth of the equally-as-large Chitina River. Only a few miles distant were the great Wrangell Mountains. These mountains were something to behold. I had seen many mountains in my flying travels, but the nearby Wrangells topped them all for grandeur and greatness. Many of the highest peaks in North America are in the Wrangells, at least three of them topping 16,000 feet. Mt. Mckinley—probably better known as Denali—in the Alaska Range was higher than twenty thousand feet; the highest peak in North America. But the Wrangells had so many great mountains; even though not quite as high, they topped the list in greatness and grandeur. I had been lucky to land in this part of the country. I knew I would like it.

Cordova Airlines had a mail contract with the U.S. Postal Department to deliver weekly mail to some of the old diggings in the Wrangells. This included the ghost town of McCarthy near what had been the great Kennicott Copper mines, until the mines had closed down in 1938. The Copper River and Northwest Railroad had served these communities during the mining days, but the railroad was now abandoned as well, and there were no roads in that country. It was necessary to fly if you wanted to get somewhere. Since flying was my business, this was right down my alley. I became the mail pilot with stops at several communities in the Wrangells, in addition to McCarthy. This afforded me an opportunity to get to know the country as well as the Alaska residents that still lived in these outlying areas. I became a very avid, interested learner.

A mail run in 1955 for Cordova Airlines.

My flights with the mail took me right through the heart of the Wrangells. I started to learn the name and location of every drainage, every valley, and every peak that was named. I used a sectional map constantly and also had put a wall map up in the cabin I occupied in Chitina. In time I would get to know the country probably better than anyone else. That is where I started learning about the white Dall sheep. There were hundreds of them on the mountains I cruised over; easily seen from the air due to the contrast of their white color against the darker color of their habitat. I often counted herds of up to 200 ewes and lambs and it was not unusual to see bunches of over 40 rams. I soon learned that the rams do not mix with the ewes until the rutting season in late fall.

The mail run afforded me a way to get acquainted with old-timers in the outlying mail stops. These old fellows, as well as more of them at my base at Chitina, had been active prospectors and were very knowledgeable about the country. They were interesting to listen to with tales of bygone experiences on their quest for minerals. They knew enough about prospecting to recognize any mineral that might be found, not just gold alone. Since there had been a great copper mine at Kennicott, they prospected for more copper; it being possible to sell claims to Kennicott if they located a good copper claim. They looked for, and noticed, all kinds of minerals that might exist in enough abundance to have some value.

These old men knew of Dall sheep, also, since the sheep were numerous on the mountains they prospected. Thus, I listened when they told me about sheep and in what drainage they had found them. This was good information for me. At times I would "prime" these fellows with a six pack of beer to help get them telling stories. Then I kept my own mouth shut and listened, getting facts. At times, if one of them ran down a bit, about all I needed to do was ask a leading question to get him started again.

All the information I was getting was going into my head and was fine. It is too bad, however, that I did not take notes as we went along. Memory alone does not last as it should, so a lot of the stuff I learned faded back out of my memory as time went on. Yet luckily, a lot of it was retained enough so that I had most of the basic knowledge I needed to know about the country.

The mail run was surely handy for getting around and getting to see what I was looking for. I was looking for more Dall sheep and places where it might be possible for me to land an airplane and hunt them. I varied my flight course on every trip so I could see more of the country. I looked closely at each valley that might have a place where an airplane might land. Older pilots had looked this country over very good with the same thought in mind, but for the most part, they had done very little about it; so in the 1950s not too many landing spots were known of.

Landing strips to access sheep hunting were made by clearing just enough brush to land safely. These strips are known to only seasoned bush pilots.

Cordova Airlines knew of a few spots where older pilots had landed. They told me to look these places over since I could drop off hunters in the valleys below mountains where Dall sheep were hanging out. Some of these places were on gravel bars on the rivers or on natural meadows that offered suitable terrain for a safe landing. Their knowledge was spotty, however, so they did not have very many places for me to take sheep hunters. I wanted to find more safe places to land and knew that if I stuck with it, in time, I would.

Even in the 1950s there were beginning to be a lot of sheep hunters—more of them every year. The Dall sheep were the most coveted of all North America big game trophies and many wanted to hunt them. I knew there would be more of them every year, with not actually realizing where it all might end some day. I just knew there would be more hunters each year and that it was time to get prepared for them.

Already there was a saying that if a person had an airplane, the information where to find sheep, and the ability to land there, he need never worry about having ready customers—they would come to him. And they did—as I was to find out the first year I started taking resident hunters in. Residents could hunt without a guide and started coming hot and heavy. These were called "fly-in" hunts, which is exactly what they were. All the pilot had to do was the flying and probably choose the spot for them to hunt. He dropped the hunters off and had an agreement with them on what day to pick them up and return them to his base.

Some of these fly-in hunters were pure novices and had no firm idea of just how to go about hunting sheep and were, for a great part, unsuccessful. They were just learning and it was costing them for the knowledge, but many of them did learn.

Some of them, however, were already good sheep hunters and knew what they were about. Generally these fellows got the trophies—and such trophies they were! Beautiful, full curl rams. Something to marvel about and also to learn about. If I was to hunt these things—and I knew I would—then seeing these already taken by other hunters helped a great deal for future knowledge. I was learning. Hunters are always willing and glad to tell how they went about their hunt; how they climbed, how they stalked their game, and information about just what they were looking for in a head to make sure they were getting a truly valued animal. I listened and learned and ask questions and learned more.

Fly-in hunts became more and more common in the '50s and '60s. Andy Runyon and the author look over trophies from a 1959 hunt.

I soon learned just what a full curl ram was, versus one of only three-quarter curl, etc. And I learned about the rings on the horns which tell the age of the ram. Each year, during the summer months, the horns on a wild sheep grow a small amount. This growth occurs each summer for the entire life of the animal. During the winter months the growth stops, or at least slows down. A ring is thus formed around the horn each year which can be seen and counted to determine the age of the animal. At about the age of eight years the horns reach a full curl. All this knowledge, plus a lot more, registered and helped for future reference. I wanted to be able to tell my hunters as much as possible about the animal they were going to hunt so they could really appreciate their trophies. Of course, some of the hunters knew a lot more than I did, so that helped a lot.

Sheep were not the only animals to consider. If a person was going to become a guide and possibly an outfitter for big game hunts, it was necessary to diversify. So I studied the great moose and caribou herds in Alaska as well. It was, and still is, a great country for big game. There were numerous grizzly and black bear to be hunted and there were mountain goats in some areas. Therefore, a person could be a very busy man during the somewhat short big game seasons. Sheep season started on August tenth each year and ended on September twentieth. The moose and caribou seasons were very similar so the rest of the year was devoted to the charter business and had nothing to do with hunting. All animals were hunted at some time or other so it was sometimes rather tricky getting everything scheduled so there was time to hunt each species. I handled these hunts as well as possible, given the circumstances that I was working for an airline and taking orders from more than one boss—with sometimes conflicting orders. It was impossible to please everybody in the hunting business, fly the mail, and do whatever else one of my bosses wanted. So I looked forward to a time when I could become independent and do it all my own way. Within three years, in late 1956, the time finally came.

I was able to resign and buy my own airplane at that time with help from O.A. Nelson of Chitina. He wanted to see the town have its own air service. That was how I got started as an independent operator. It took a lot of hard work and time, but I was able to pay for the airplane eventually by taking every charter that came my way. I also needed to hunt as much as possible in the autumn months for the sheep and moose that I was beginning to know so well in the Wrangell Mountain area. It was now possible to take on a guided hunt at times, as well as the local fly-in hunts. My knowledge of this profession increased steadily as time went on.

Over the years since the early 1950s I became an experienced sheep guide and hunter. Each year there were more hunts and knowledge was gained on each one. In time I became known as one of the better guides and more successful than some of the others. I acquired more business than I could handle and it was necessary to turn down many requests for sheep hunts. I just could not become too crowded to the point that I wouldn't have enough time to conduct either a fly-in hunt or a guided one. I selected my hunters carefully; then took on just enough of them so I could handle everything properly, and still take enough time to get each hunt completed successfully. This was a satisfying profession. I was doing just what I had wanted to do. I knew this was to be my way of life until I became too old to do it any more.

Each species of big game was hunted at one time or another, but with some overlap. Here are three trophy sheep horns and a black bear hide.

During this time we learned more about the sheep and their ages. We found that by counting the rings on the horns of trophies taken that a ram reaches a full curl at about eight years of age. We also learned that they seldom get more that 12 years old before they die. In time the ram's teeth wear down and some of the lower teeth in the front of the mouth drop out. Then the ram cannot get enough to eat to sustain the rigorous life they lead. This factor hastens their death from starvation. There are cases of them living to the age of fourteen years, but generally speaking, a ram's life ends at somewhere around twelve years.

Reading naturalists' reports verified this fact, and others, and added to our general knowledge of sheep. I took advantage of these facts we were learning. Some of us together reasoned out the fact that it would always be best to take full curl rams only, instead of including three-quarter rams—which at that time were legal to take in Alaska.

The reasoning went on from that point. We had learned that the three-quarter curl rams were old enough and perfectly capable of breeding the ewes when the fall rutting season came. Thus, in theory, if hunters took full curl rams only and let the three-quarter curls go, the herd's strength in numbers should remain the same. As long as hunting pressure did not increase to a dangerous level there would always—for all times—be a herd that was as big as when the hunting began. The full curl rams were somewhat already past their prime and were going to die within just a few short years, so it would not hurt the herd one bit to kill them off as time went on and more of them got to the full curl stage.

The true trophy hunters did not want, nor ever considered shooting, less than a full curl ram. Yet some of the novice fly-in hunters were prone to shoot the first legal ram they saw, which included the three-quarter curls. I took it upon myself to try to train them differently before their hunt began. I explained about this full curl theory and that they should just hunt a little harder and let the smaller rams go. Then they could wind up with a full curl, have a much better trophy, and also the population of the herd would remain the same. Sometimes this worked and sometimes it did not. At any rate I believed I was doing some good at least.

In a few short years my business was quite well established. During the hunting season in August and September I could devote a good bit of my time to the hunting business, mostly with the Dall sheep, and some with moose, caribou, and grizzly bear. The rest of the year, except the most bitter cold times during the months of December and January, was devoted to charter. Chartering was very diversified and there was plenty of flying, since competition was not very fierce. I was a busy, but happy, man.

Other guides and outfitters showed up and hunted in the Wrangells and I no longer had the sheep hunts so much to myself. Some of these outfitters did part of, or all of, their flying themselves; some did not. We decided that rather than fight this competition we would, instead, join them. So we established a business of using our larger airplanes to fly to the airline terminal in Anchorage to pick up their nonresident hunters. We flew these hunters out to Gulkana Airfield where my new base was, having left Chitina in 1959. In Gulkana we transferred them to smaller planes and flew them out to their outfitter's base camp in the Wrangell Mountains.

I liked to guide hunters and took on as many guided hunts as possible, which were not very many actually. I hired a couple of guides and became an outfitter as well. Most of my time seemed to be devoted to flying those aircraft, which I loved, but it was nice to guide a hunter whenever I could arrange to take the proper time for it. I hired another competent pilot to fly the larger aircraft and handle the flights to the airline terminals in either Anchorage or Fairbanks; and to take care of other charter flights which came up. It was all working out quite well since the very young pilot I hired, Mike Stone, was an extremely competent and safe pilot.

Elmer Rasmussen's grand slam of North American wild sheep: Clockwise from upper left—Dall sheep, Stone sheep, desert bighorn, and Rocky Mountain bighorn.

CHAPTER 3
THE WILD SHEEP OF NORTH AMERICA

The white sheep, Ovis dalli dalli, range in Alaska, the Yukon Territory, and the Northwest Territories. Also in the Yukon and British Columbia there are Stone sheep, Ovis dalli stonei. The Stone sheep are dark colored, sometimes nearly black. Both the Stone and the Dall are known as *thinhorn* sheep in contrast to the *bighorn* sheep—which range further south. There is also another thinhorn sheep known as the Fannin which, it is claimed, is merely another color phase of the Dall. Although their colors vary, sometimes they may have white legs and chests, but their backs will be grey. The old-timers called these "Saddlebacks." For a long time people believed Fannins were a result of crossbreeding between the Stone sheep and the Dall, but apparently this is not so. The Fannin sheep are not numerous and only a very few occur in Alaska.

In British Columbia there is a gap in the Rocky Mountains extending for perhaps 150 miles where there are no sheep. From that point south through the Canadian Rockies, through the United States, and on down into old Mexico is the range of the bighorn sheep and its various subspecies.

Canadian bighorns, Ovis canadensis canadensis, range down through British Columbia through the States and on down into old Mexico. Other subspecies of the bighorn range through Washington and

California. There is also the desert bighorn which can be located in Arizona and Sonora. The range of the bighorn covers a lot of territory.

Due to the gap between the Dall and Stone sheep in the north and the bighorn further south, there is no interbreeding between the thinhorns and the bighorns.

It is very interesting to note the adaptability of the wild sheep to different climatic conditions. Here we have Dall sheep very numerous in the furthest north mountain range in Alaska—the Brooks range. Here there is darkness for nearly half the year, bitter cold, and winter storms that howl across the steep slopes. Yet these same storms remove the snow from the slopes and expose feed. The sheep with their warm hair and wool live and feed through the winter and survive. The range of the sheep extends south from the Brooks Range clear down into the deserts of Mexico, where sheep have adapted themselves very well to this extremely hot climate. Sheep do not care for damp climates, however, and are not found on ranges which border on the ocean. They prefer the dryer interior.

Wild sheep do not have wool such as their very distant relative, the domestic sheep. Sheep have hair which is hollow, forming perfect insulation. In the far north they also grow a thin layer of very fine wool next to their skin, which further insulates their body against cold. This is why, if you fly past and observe the sheep in winter, you will see them grazing on slopes where hardly any other animal could survive. They rest in and under rimrocks and overhangs which are protected from the bitter winds. There is no other animal which can adapt to such extreme climatic conditions as the sheep. The grizzly bear runs a close second, however.

In Alaska there are Dall sheep on each and every one of the various mountain ranges. This takes some consideration and thought since

Alaska itself is such a vast country. Some people have a difficult time in determining just how large Alaska is. Briefly, Alaska is probably about twice the size of Texas—which is the largest state in the contiguous 48 states. Alaska is one-fifth the size of the entire United States. There are thousands of miles of shoreline. There are several mountain ranges and at least parts of each of these great mountain systems have bands of Dall sheep on them.

To get a good idea of how vast this country is, it is good to have a map of the state of Alaska which shows the mountain ranges. Then we may start from the north and work our way southward.

Stone sheep along a road in British Columbia. Stone and Dall sheep are both called thinhorn sheep because of their (relatively) slender horns.

The Brooks Range will be first. From the Northwest Territories on the east this range extends clear across Alaska to the Arctic Ocean. On the north side of the range is the beginning of the true Arctic. Our farthest north city, Barrow is on the coast a goodly distance north of the Brooks Range. Here are the great Prudhoe Bay oilfields as well. There are no sheep on the north slope of the Brooks Range.

However, on the south slope there are numerous bands of sheep in parts of the range. These Brooks Range sheep are slightly different than those on the more southerly ranges and their horns do not grow quite as big. However they are perfectly formed, beautiful amber-colored horns and are seldom broomed off. They are fine trophies for the hunter which does not necessarily desire a record book trophy.

Further south across the great Yukon Basin is the Alaska Range, which connects up with the St. Elias Mountains in Alaska and the Yukon Territory. The Alaska Range runs westerly, then in a great arc turns nearly south past our highest peak, Mt. McKinley; then extends on southward until it peters out at the beginning of the Alaska Peninsula. There are Dall sheep on both sides of the Alaska Range and, considering its great length and breadth, that means a lot of sheep.

Between the Alaska Range and the Anchorage Bowl are the Talkeetna Mountains. These mountains are not quite so high and rugged as the other ranges, but take in a lot of territory and harbor Dall sheep in many places.

Next come the Chugach Mountains—the great coastal barrier which has so much to do with the climate in southcentral Alaska. The Chugaches extend eastward along the southern coast from the Anchorage area until they merge into the St. Elias mountains near the eastern border. On the south side of the Chugach Mountains we have the very wet coastal climate, where it rains much more than it snows. There are no sheep on the coastal side where the wet weather occurs. However, on the north side there is some fine sheep country and some of the largest trophies have come from the Chugaches.

Then we have the great Wrangell Mountains in central Alaska. The Wrangells, jutting out from the St. Elias Mountains in a great bulge, are the most magnificent mountains in the entire state. Here there are great icefields around the Mt. Wrangell massif, which has a semi-active volcano on its top. There are more mountains here over 16,000 feet than any other range in North America. But there is much more than just icefields. In its vast expanse there are many mountains that are perfect for Dall sheep. I have always believed, and still do, that there are more sheep in the Wrangells than any other mountain range in the state. The World Record Dall ram came from the Wrangells, a feat in which I was directly involved, though as the supposed guide rather than the hunter.

The Chugach Mountains produce many large sheep each season like these two heavy-horned rams .

There are sheep on the Kenai Peninsula and there are also sheep in the White Mountains and the Tanana Hills north of the Yukon River. There we pretty well have it. There are quite possibly more sheep in Alaska than there are in all the other sheep country combined, but that is not proven. It has been impossible to get an accurate count on just how many sheep there are due to the rugged terrain they occupy. However, it has been estimated that there are between 30,000 and 50,000 sheep in Alaska. That is probably the best figure on how many sheep there are. It is partly a guess, but is based on good knowledge.

Lambs are usually born on cliffs where few predators can go. Once the lambs can run, ewes will move to green slopes to feed.

In Alaska the lambs are born mostly during the month of June. By that time all the snow is gone at the lower elevations, the sun is warm, and everything is getting green. The lower slopes of the mountains start getting green growth first and the sheep move down to the lower elevations to take advantage of the new feed. That is where the lambs are usually born.

It is possible to observe the sheep at the lower elevations quite easily. I learned to do that and many times have landed on a river bar to observe them. It is a joy to be out there in the beautiful setting and enjoy the wonderful early summer weather. It is best to have a spotting scope or at least field glasses to see what is going on in the sheep world above.

The newborn lambs soon learn to get around in their natural habitat quite as well as their mothers. They run and gambol and play in bunches and cause their mothers to get distraught and chase after them, but it seemingly does no good. The lambs, in their natural element amid the rocks and extremely steep slopes, run and play with abandon. A lamb will certainly run to its mother within awhile, however, and suck to get milk to keep it going some more; then it's off again to play with the other lambs.

I have flown others out with me to see this show more than once; since it is such a worthwhile thing to see and something very few people in the world have observed. The green growth rapidly appears higher on the mountain and the sheep go up with it until they are very high, up to probably the 6,000 foot level. By that time the show is over and the sheep go to their summer pastures, where they cannot be so easily observed from below.

The rams often come down the mountain to the lower elevations, too, so they can also partake of the new, green feed. They seldom mix with the ewes and remain in their separate area, but they can also be observed through a spotting scope. I noticed them very carefully and looked at them with a hunter's eye to evaluate their horn value for future hunting. I looked at them as a rancher might look at his cattle to see how the autumn harvest might be.

It was the beautiful country which I could never see enough of, as well as the sheep themselves which I could enjoy at that time of year.

Sheep are not migratory animals. A sheep born on a certain set of mountains will likely remain within that range all his life. The rams roam farther than the ewes do, but still remain within that certain range. They move around during the summer months and often can be seen in the same area they were seen in the previous years. In this respect, they are similar to moose, which also do not typically migrate very far from their place of birth during their lifetime.

There is no way a novice sheep hunter can learn how to hunt sheep successfully by just sitting down and listening to how it is done. The only way it can be learned is by experience. Therefore, it is wise to have a guide. If the hunter is a resident of Alaska he can go with a friend who has hunted sheep at a previous time and learned something about it. This is a very good idea. Of course a novice can learn on his own. But the knowledge is expensive if he is to pay for a hunt and then go out there and find out how it should not be done before he learns the proper precautions and methods that are successful.

Sheep are naturally wild animals and are very leery of all predators, and this certainly includes humans. Sheep have extremely good eyesight and will see the slightest movement on the mountain—even from a very great distance—and take note of it. This does not necessarily mean they will get right up and run, but it will mean they will be aware and watchful. A bunch of rams will bed down on a steep mountain slope and position themselves so they can see all points of the compass. They will take note of any movement which might become dangerous to their existence.

You can spot sheep from way down below them and it will not disturb them in the least. Just do not remain within their sight when climbing the mountain. Take a roundabout route where cover exists and get up there without being seen. When disturbed, sheep will generally go up, which means safety to them—since no other animal, except a goat, can match their pace up a mountain. Their stamina is terrific. A hunter should therefore get above, or at least up even with, the sheep before beginning the stalk. If sheep do see you climbing up toward them, they may seem deceiving.

One of the many huge rams taken from the Wrangell Mountains. Dene Leonard, Jr., took this 173 5/8 B&C ram in 1959.

They will not get up and bound away as a deer would do. Instead, they will likely get up, stretch, feed a little bit, and then start walking up the mountain at a seemingly leisurely pace. They do not hurry at all. Yet they will be going up that mountain faster then a man can follow. They will keep going until they are over the top and gone to the next mountain, or wherever it seems safest to them. So if you disturb your sheep, you may as will give up and hunt another day.

A hunter should be well-equipped when hunting sheep. Yet he should not overburden himself with equipment; since, if the hunt is successful, he will have a large amount of weight when descending the mountain. Therefore, choose the equipment with thought and take only what is absolutely necessary. I settled on carrying a plain old Trapper Nelson packboard, which is light and fairly comfortable. However, there are many packs that can be bought and it is up to the hunter as to which one he chooses. I believe all of them are reasonably light and adequate for the purpose.

Of course I had good climbing boots, which is a must, along with adequate clothing—including a jacket. My pack included a few small tools, including an extra knife. Although I carried a pocket knife and a small belt knife it is possible to lose a knife, and they weigh very little. There was also a small stone for knife sharpening. I carried a small saw—usually one called a Knapp saw—which is good for removing the horns and the top portion of the skull from the remainder of the skull. I always had field glasses, but usually left the spotting scope in camp. A spotting scope is a very handy tool, but has some weight. The field glasses will usually suffice for evaluating a ram's horns before beginning a stalk. That was a about all I wanted to carry up the mountain except, of course, some lunch for the hunter and myself.

The State of Alaska has a wanton waste law which is a very good law. It means that a hunter should take all edible portions of the meat. An exception is made for bear meat, but for all other big game animals, all the meat must be saved for human consumption. This means dressing out the carcass properly and cutting the meat up into pack-size portions for carrying down the mountain. Some hunters bone out the meat, which gets rid of some dead weight; yet I never wanted to bone out the meat if there was any way of getting it all down in large pieces. Boned meat is hard to figure out for making the proper cuts for cooking purposes. So we made it our practice to save all the meat and charge enough extra for the trouble of getting it packed out. Many guides did not do this and merely took a small portion of the meat, or sometimes none at all. These were mostly the outlaw guides who showed up and broke regulations at will, and usually got away with it. But we wanted all the meat—and sheep meat is delectable to eat. It has its own flavor and no other meat can be compared to it. I can promise if you bring the meat down you will never regret the extra effort. There is absolutely no comparison of the meat of wild sheep with that of their distant cousin, the domestic sheep. Very few people ever experience the flavor of wild sheep meat since a hunter, after packing one or two heavy loads of meat off the mountain, seldom wants to share it with anyone except his own family.

Spotting sheep from the air was usually done with a Super Cub (like this one), followed by landing hunters on a wilderness "airport" (also pictured) within walking distance of the sheep.

CHAPTER 4
SPOTTING AND LOCATING SHEEP

As the years went by I realized the country I was hunting in the Wrangells had some of the biggest and finest sheep trophies of anywhere within Alaska. It seemed that, with pure luck, I had arrived at the best place for these large trophies. Through hunting, comparing notes, and evaluating information we knew there were several herds of sheep that possibly surpassed any sheep in other parts of Alaska. Therefore, we capitalized on this fact.

I had already guided hunters in this country to record trophies. As this fact became known, it quite naturally helped the business. I was getting requests from the real trophy hunters, those men who want the largest they can get. I took advantage of that fact and started booking them on a very small scale. That was because I was a very small outfitter and could only take a very limited amount of hunters each year. I chose my hunters very carefully.

I learned early on that it was very unwise to guarantee a certain trophy. Of course there were prospective hunters who wanted to be certain they were going to get the size trophy they desired. They would naturally ask if I would "guarantee" the hunt. This I would refuse to do. The only guarantee I would give was: I knew the whereabouts of very large sheep; I could hunt them; and I would give an honest effort to produce that trophy—no more, no less. If they would not buy this, then I turned them down for the hunt.

It was very necessary for me to know just what I had in the way of sheep to hunt, just where their range was during the open season, and reasonable knowledge as to their size and numbers. So I looked at and spotted sheep on the various ranges and, of course, this was done from the air.

The Alaska Department of Fish and Game has a regulation—a very good one—that it is unlawful to herd or harass game from the air. It did not take me long to learn to abide by that regulation. If you fly close to a bunch of sheep to evaluate the size of their horns and get an accurate count of how many large rams are in the bunch, you will scare them. In fact, buzzing sheep terrorizes them. When you buzz sheep, they leave the country through fear. Since sheep nearly always go up when scared of anything, that is just what they do when buzzed by an airplane. They go completely up in the rimrocks just under the ice cap; and make no bones about it, a sheep can easily go where a human cannot follow. This is the country they live in, where they are perfectly adapted, and they can easily go where noone but an experienced high climber fully equipped with crampons, carabiners, pitons, rope, etc., can go. And they will remain up there in those rimrocks for several days, until hunger and the likelihood that they will not be buzzed again brings them back down.

Nevertheless, I did spot sheep, but in a legal manner. I just did not get close enough to scare them. I learned how close I could get and still not bother them, then never went any closer. I used field glasses to get a closer look; and, if the air was not very turbulent, I could get a pretty fair idea of what was available. This worked out very well and I usually got all the information I needed. On these flights I always flew alone, since I did not want to divulge this knowledge to another person who might talk about what we had seen. We were becoming secretive about these things.

Evaluating trophy sheep was, and is, best done from the ground.

To be sure, I had many requests from trophy hunters to go and spot sheep for them so they could evaluate the horn size and find a great trophy. They would come and practically demand that I do this for them. When I turned them down, I had offers of up to triple my regular charter rate to do the flying. I turned down all these requests, regardless of the offer, since I had learned there could not possibly be any gain in doing this thing. I tried to explain to these would-be hunters that to buzz the sheep would be to defeat their own purpose—the sheep would leave the country if we bothered them. Some of them, indignant at my refusal, said they would get another pilot to do it for them. Since every man is free and can do as he pleases in this country, all I could say was go ahead and get another pilot. Some of them did. There definitely were other pilots available who, through not caring if they broke the regulation, or possibly without knowing they were doing a useless thing, would go ahead and fly out there and terrorize the sheep.

Sheep country airstrip on the Chetaslina River; Mt. Wrangell Massif in the background.

CHAPTER 5
BUILDING THE AIRSTRIPS

As stated before, I had looked from the air for places where an airplane might land near the base of the mountains for the purpose of hunting sheep. To be successful in this operation we would need several airstrips and I was determined to get it done as time went on. I had no idea, nor did I even think of it at the time, what the repercussions would be in the future by creating these airstrips. I just wanted to get it done and started working at it.

I had already made a couple more airstrips up near the headwaters of the Chitina River. In one place I had landed out in the middle of the wide river valley on a good gravel bar. Then I had waded through the various braided channels of the river for a couple miles until I reached a place near the mountain and the timber, a very attractive place where there was plenty of firewood and adequate water. This one had not been much trouble since it was a natural place to land anyway, although I could not tell that from the air. It merely meant I needed to grub out some small brush, remove some driftwood, then mark the place so it could be seen from the air—and there we had it. I had also managed to land up in the "Slot" about three miles above the terminus of the Chitina Glacier without damaging my airplane. Then it took a lot of brush removal, getting rid of rotten logs, and some ground work filling holes and removing a few rocks.

These were prime places because we recognized that the sheep on the upper Chitina had larger horns than any other known spot in the Wrangells. I knew we would have good hunting from these airstrips as time went on.

We wanted more, though. We desired a place that was really remote and that would offer a great deal of hunting. As I searched the valley of the south side of the Wrangells that I hunted in, I found the place.

Natural airstrips like this one high in the Wrangells were available for adventuresome pilots like Jack Wilson. Other airstrips had to be built.

It was only a short flight from my base at Chitina to this chosen place. The Chetaslina River begins at the base of Mt. Wrangell and flows westward to its confluence with the Copper River. The east fork of this river runs parallel to the main fork, with a mountain in between, until it merges. Then to the north is Chichokna Creek, which also drains into the main Chetaslina. In the mountains between these drainages there were many, many sheep; more sheep than I had seen anywhere else and it appeared that they had never been hunted. Not recently at any rate. Old prospectors who had roamed that country had probably killed meat for subsistence, but that had been years ago and the sheep now existing had never been hunted.

I wondered if this sheep range was overstocked with animals. That was a possibility since many animals do overstock their range; then, at the top of a cycle, die off until there are very few animals left. Then, as nature has arranged these things, the herd very slowly builds back up again. Since there had never been a study made where overstocking was possibly happening on a sheep range, I had no knowledge if this was occurring with the sheep between these drainages. I just knew there was a great amount of sheep here and I wanted to hunt them.

Finding a good spot for an airstrip was the problem. I cruised the valleys slowly at low altitude and looked them over closely. The main branch of the river was the most centrally located, but the river bars were covered with boulders and a lot of brush. The upper Chichokna had fairly good possibilities, however. This was above timberline, and trees and brush would not be much problem. There was a tundra-covered bar high enough above the stream that flooding would probably not be a bother, and level enough for the purpose. It was covered with heavy tundra, which would have to be removed. This tundra, at a depth of about six inches, was soft and would cause enough drag on the wheels to nose the airplane over, and we could not have that.

Harley King and I sat down and planned it all out. Harley, a resident of Cordova, was a guide and a good sportsman. He was also a pilot, although his experience was limited. We teamed up on this project and decided to do it together. The next step would be getting

Harley in there where he could start work on an airstrip.

There was no place anywhere near to land an airplane, but we had to find a spot. We finally decided on Dadina lake, which is situated between the mountains and the Copper River, and bordered with large spruce timber. It was sixteen miles from the lake to the spot we wanted the strip, yet Harley said he would be glad to do it. So with a pack containing a few days food and his rifle, I dropped him off with a floatplane and he started for the mountain. We figured it would take him two days to reach the Chichokna River near the mouth of Sheep Gulch where we wanted the strip.

The Sheep Gulch airstrip provided some easy hunting for many years; here are two guides, two hunters, and their trophies.

I flew the wheelplane up to our site and dropped some tools—including a grubbing hoe, a shovel, and a couple sharp axes. Then I waited a couple days for Harley to got there. After he arrived I dropped food for him, then waited a few days for him to work on it. This was getting to be quite an enterprise.

Finally, it looked like I could make a landing and did so. But there was not enough tundra removed as yet, so the airplane slowed down and went right up on its nose! Luckily, there was no damage since my speed was slowed down enough to prevent that. So we moved the airplane up the creek a small distance to a better place and started working like slaves to remove that tundra. We knew it was going to take quite a bit of time. Yet we felt the result would be very good.

We had a very exciting experience the next morning, however. We had bedded down in the open near a small stream and slept right on the soft tundra. I arose at about six the next morning, got out and took the coffee pot to the creek to fill it. Suddenly, I heard Harley say, "Look out, Jack! Look out!" I looked his way and there he was, standing in his shorts with his rifle at the ready, while down toward the airstrip there was a large grizzly bear charging us! She was coming at us like a freight train, followed by two small cubs. My movements had disturbed her and she probably thought her cubs were in danger from us.

I ran around behind Harley and said, "Shoot the old son-of-a-bitch, shoot!" But Harley—a calm, efficient man—said, "Not yet, Jack. Not yet." She continued on until she was within thirty feet, but then she broke it off, hopped the creek, and ran up a high bank. Then she turned around and came at us again, and once more I said "Shoot her!" But Harley—still calm and ready—said, "Not yet, Jack." Luckily, she broke it off again, and she and the cubs hopped back across the little creek and took off down the valley. Such excitement! I was very relieved and had been terrified. Yet Harley had handled the situation very well with his calm actions. I asked him why he did not just shoot her. He said he just couldn't shoot a bear with cubs, but if she had come past a certain bush he was using as at marker, he would have done so.

So much for that. I was nervous all day as we worked. Then we had a pleasant diversion. A bunch of rams moved in close, under the lower rimrocks on the steep hillside above us, bedded down, and watched us. They were not over two hundred yards from us, and we could have easily shot one. We did not want to do that, however. It was against regulations to hunt out of season and we did not need fresh meat badly anyway. But I thought of how nice it would be with a hunter and these sheep so tame. There were so many sheep in this country. It was a wonderful thing to us.

In time we had the strip improved enough so I could safely land there, and Harley would be able to land there as well. We cropped our sheep, trying to never over-hunt it. We had some good hunts, both with nonresident guided hunts and with fly-in hunts. Over a number of years we had some easy hunting and there were three directions to go to find sheep in plentiful numbers.

In time, the sheep hunting in that beautiful setting did die down some. Other guides and private pilots built strips on nearby drainages and could reach some of our "herd." For the most part, others did not try to use our airstrip which we had worked so hard to build, yet there were a few that did. So when we were not there hunting, I did set up a camp to leave, thinking that might help keep others away; but it did not work out too well. This was real bear country as well as sheep country and bears love to tear up a tent and make a mess of all that is included with it. We did not want to shoot the bear since they are trophy animals, too. A bear is worth a lot of money to a guide. We put up with them, which was a gain to us later, although I never did a great deal of bear hunting. Harley was a much better bear guide than I.

Over the years the sheep population in Sheep Gulch and the nearby mountains did diminish, although we took only full curl rams— never taking the three-quarter curls. This apparently bore out my theory that the range was overstocked with sheep, because the population crashed.

Some of my fondest memories of the sheep hunting years are of our airstrip near Sheep Gulch. It was the most ideal setup of all the places we hunted. For fly-in hunters we chose only those who we knew were good sportsmen and that would shoot nothing except the full curls. It seemed that all our guided hunters turned out to be the same kind of people. Although there was no timber, there was enough brush for a campfire, so we had many good meals and enjoyable evenings with a campfire. Many stories were told.

A few lakes were suitable as drop-off points for sheep hunters, like this one in Skolai Basin.

There were other airstrips. We found that we could land on certain mountaintops which were smooth enough and level enough for that purpose. Then the place could be improved and runway markers set up. On these mountaintop strips we had to be very careful. Dangerous winds at the high altitude could come up rapidly. Sometimes cloud cover obscured the mountain for several days, preventing flights either in or out. We were within the law, all right, to have these places, as long as we established a camp and remained there overnight before beginning the hunt. But it was devastating for the sheep. It very naturally made it easier to get them from these places. It can be argued that it was entirely wrong and not sporting at all. I knew that was a sound argument with a lot of merit. Yet we did it anyway. In the Old West men had exploited the riches of the new country with a will, and we were no different. As long as there was no law against a lucrative enterprise we did it—whether right or wrong.

Every valley from which numerous sheep could be reached was looked over for the possibility of building an airstrip. I was not alone in this. There were more guides each year who had their own airplanes and many people in Alaska had aircraft. A lot of private pilots showed up with Super Cubs or other small, good-performing aircraft and started hunting in the Wrangells. Many of these people built their own airstrips. As stated before, I did not fight these other people moving into what had seemed to be my own country, since I knew it would be useless to do so. Instead, I did some of the flying for them.

There was a place called Hidden Creek that I wanted to get into, since there were both goats and sheep in that drainage. But it seemed impossible to ever get in there. The name "Hidden Creek" was no misnomer. It really was hidden from access, although it could be seen from the air. It drained into the great Kennicott Glacier above McCarthy. It had been explored by the old time prospectors. They had climbed over rugged mountains from the southwest, but nobody thought that was a very worthwhile way to get in, since it was a treacherous trip.

From the glacier side, Hidden Creek had a lake which was formed by glacial movement. As the glacier flowed slowly down, as glaciers do, it blocked the entrance to the valley. The creek formed a formidable-looking lake with many icebergs in it. Each year this lake built up to a great body of water and remained there, blocking access to the valley. During the hot summer months after it had built up high enough, water could finally escape over the ice and wear it away. Then, suddenly, the whole mass of ice blocking the valley let go at once.

Photo courtesy of Georgia Strunk.

A large sheep mount from the 1950s.

This caused flooding in a rush. The water rushed down under the glacier, then came out at the terminus just opposite McCarthy. When this happens the Kennicott River was, and is, a great raging torrent. It still happens every year at some unpredictable time in summer. When it floods, water shoots out 30 feet in the air from under the glacier, then tears on down the river. Great icebergs calve from the glacier and flow down the river. That is why there is no road to the town of McCarthy. Bridges have been built at the Kennicott River, but ice has always taken them out. So the residents of the town devised a unique system. They built a cable tram across the river and bring the many tourists over to the town by that means. It seems to work all right and many tourists love it. During the winter months vehicles can cross the river on the ice, so residents get their year's supply of gasoline and supplies across for the next year by that means.

Hidden Creek was inaccessible, but there was a man who wanted to get in there for the purpose of hunting and he had the means. He was the party chief for a mineral exploration company and they used a helicopter. Helicopters were coming along stronger all the time and were being used extensively for mineral exploration. The helicopter could, of course, land at Hidden Creek. This geologist asked me to show them how to build a strip so he could go sheep hunting that fall after his job was finished. I agreed to go right along and not only show them how, but to stay and help.

Late one evening we went into Hidden Creek and located a spot with good possibilities. It was very boulder-strewn in there, but there was one good spot and we went to work on it—removing rocks, filling holes, and generally leveling it up. We worked until very late that night, but the long summer daylight hours we have in Alaska stayed with us and we got the job done.

That fall I took the hunter in and he got both a sheep and a goat without a great deal of trouble and was extremely pleased.

So I now had another airstrip with great plans for using it, but it never worked out very well. There had been a certain amount of publicity connected with building this strip, it became well known, and other pilots "helped" me hunt the place. I finally just gave the place up after a couple years when it became crowded.

BUILDING THE AIRSTRIPS 55

Photo courtesy of Georgia Strunk.

Having a camera within reach at all times will eventually reward you with an outstanding wildlife photo.

CHAPTER 6
THE GRAVITY TESTER

After several years as a busy bush pilot and guide in Alaska, there had been enough success that I was getting along very well. I had no trouble paying my bills. I was getting to know this great beautiful country very well and liked it more than I could say. I was satisfied being a professional pilot and part-time guide, yet there is always something else a man can do and become. I had it in my mind to become a wildlife photographer, along with all my other activities.

The main trouble here—as I certainly found out later—was that it took a lot more than a person thinks to become a good wildlife photographer. I had no idea just what it took and did not know a thing about photography. Certainly I could take a group photo or a picture of one of my clients with a trophy, yet I did not have the foggiest notion of what it takes to become a successful photographer of our great wild game herds. I just figured I could certainly learn. Basically, I had no idea of what kind of equipment I would need. I could learn that, as time went on, certainly; but I did not realize how much time this business would take. I suppose I thought I could take a day off, go up on a likely mountain, and come back that evening with beautiful close-up photos of great Dall rams and ewes. I did not know that it takes a whale of a lot more than that. Such photography takes not only a good knowledge of the equipment needed, and how it was to be operated, but it takes time. And a great deal of time at that. To get good pictures, it takes the patience of Job to get close enough to the subject, with same subject in the right position to get a good picture. Hunting with a rifle to shoot a trophy is easy compared to this. With a rifle the guide needs to get his hunter into a position within, perhaps, one hundred yards of the trophy. Then it can be taken with an accurate shot and that is that. With photography, however, you must get much closer to the game—very much closer, which is not easily done. In days gone by, an Apache Indian was known to have great patience, lying concealed until the white man showed himself—then he could take the scalp. But I was to learn that a wildlife photographer had to have more patience than any Apache that ever lived in order to lie in wait until a subject was posed properly for a good picture.

It never did come to pass that I was to become a good wildlife photographer. Perhaps it was just a dream. As a busy pilot I could not take the time for another enterprise. I must keep going at something I knew how to do properly, and there was really not time for anything else.

I did carry a camera at all times in my Super Cub, however. It was right under my seat in a very handy place and always loaded with film and ready to go. Mostly, I used it to take a picture or two of a client after he had gotten a good trophy—with him posed alongside the airplane. There was a double purpose here. I could have the film developed, then send a print to the client as a token of good will. Also, since he would be posed by my airplane, my name on the fuselage could be plainly seen: Wilson Air Service, Gulkana Airfield. This was good advertising for a possible future client.

In 1962 1 received a radio call from the Arctic Institute of North America to come over into the Yukon Territory and help them out with an airplane. The Arctic Institute along with the National Geographic Society maintained a large camp on the east end of the great Kluane Lake, with many different kinds of scientists working from there in many directions during the summer months. Their main upper camp was on what was called the Divide between the great Kaskawulsh Glacier on the Canadian side and the Logan Glacier, which drained toward, and into, Alaska. From this high camp at the 8000 foot level they spread out in all directions, doing whatever scientists do, studying everything that could be studied up on the ice. They were making more accurate maps of the great, tremendous St. Elias icefields—by far the greatest icefields in North America.

Every plane was suited for specific jobs; the Super Cub was the best for transporting sheep hunters—like this lady hunter and her trophy.

They had their own pilot, Phil Upton, who flew a turbocharged Helio Courier-type airplane. He got them to the Divide and other camps, and kept them supplied with food and necessities. Phil was busy at it and doing a good job. However, at times they needed another kind of airplane to do certain little jobs. Each type of light aircraft had its own special uses. Although the Helio Courier could haul a big load or up to three passengers, it could not be slowed down as much as a Super Cub and was not nearly as maneuverable. The Cub could only haul one passenger along with needed gear, but could land and take off within a very small space. Also, it was much lighter and could be handled more easily on the ground. The Arctic Institute knew the Cub would be the better airplane for one of their needs.

Super Cubs are unique planes, recognizable by their great wingspan.

When they called on the radio they said they wanted me to come over, take a man who had a gravity meter up, and do some flying for him. Well, what is a gravity meter?, I wondered. I figured I could find out and, since my business was flying, I agreed to do the job. We set up a certain day when I would be able to go over there for however long it would take, and that is all I knew about the upcoming job.

At the big base camp at Kluane I met the man who had the gravity meter. I was to learn that the meter was encased in a cylinder like a short piece of stovepipe; it was an extremely sensitive instrument that would test the gravity at any location; and this had never been done in this part of the Yukon Territory. He said he needed to take a test at each thousand foot level up to as high as I could get him. This meant landing at each thousand foot interval and then waiting for the sensitive instrument to settle down. After being leveled it took about one half hour for it to settle down so a gravity reading could be taken. Such is scientific work. I still do not know anything about a gravity meter nor how the test was made. Only the scientist knew that, which was all that really mattered. I did not need to know anything more about it.

I was told he had already gotten readings up to the four thousand foot level and needed to start from that altitude. I was equipped with hydraulic wheel-skis and could land on the icefields at any level up to about the fourteen thousand foot level—which was as high as the Cub could operate. Even then, I needed very good weather and very favorable winds to get up that high and make a successful landing, followed by a successful takeoff after the job was done.

The only problem was that since this was the month of July, there was no snow at the five thousand foot level. This would mean I could not land on the skis at this altitude. From about the 6000 foot level on up I could land on the ice. But I would have to fly and look for a suitable, safe place to land at 5000 feet with the skis retracted. All we could do was go look and try to find a good place to land. We decided to try it and see if it could be done.

We flew up the right side of the Slim River since the hills were big and rolling and might offer an opportunity. At 5000 feet there seemed to be no good spot to land, but on up at nearly 6000 feet there appeared a quite level, smooth, pasture-like place that looked all right after a careful inspection at very slow speed and low altitude.

I told the scientist I could land here all right, but it would be higher than he would want for the reading. He said that was okay and that he could walk back down to the lower altitude, so we landed.

On final approach I saw a bunch of Dall sheep grazing perhaps half a mile away, above a small ledge. These were ewes and lambs and they were not disturbed. We were in the Kluane Game Preserve and hunting was not allowed. The sheep did not seem to be nervous at all about our presence and grazed along, quite tame.

"The sheep did not seem to be nervous at all about our presence and grazed along, quite tame."

I parked the airplane perhaps fifty feet from a very large boulder—as wide as a cabin, but not nearly as high. The scientist got his meter and a rifle and said he would start walking back down to the 5000 foot level for his reading. I had a new sensitive altimeter in this aircraft and gave him an accurate reading of the altitude. He carried a small altimeter on a string around his neck and set it with my very accurate one, then he was on his way. I knew it would take perhaps two hours before he returned. He did not ask me to go with him so I decided to just remain with the airplane.

I walked around for awhile, marveling at the small flowers that were growing in that beautiful setting as well as the superb scenery. Though I had spent quite a lot of time in both Alaska and the Yukon, I always appreciated the wonderful scenery in the mountains. I marveled at the plant growth and the outright beauty of the great, wonderful setting in this country I had chosen for my life.

I climbed up on that boulder, which was smooth on top, and since the sun was very warm, it was comfortable up there. I rolled up my jacket for a pillow and laid down. In a short time I had fallen asleep.

In perhaps half an hour I woke up and there were sounds nearby, noises I could not define. I turned my head to the right and there were those sheep! They had grazed right over there and were all around me. Although sheep have very good noses as well as superior eyesight, they did not pay any attention to my odor. Miraculously, they did not mind the airplane either. Airplanes are smelly things. The sheep could probably detect the smell of the residual heat in the engine. An airplane smells of oil, gasoline, and other assorted odors. Even I, a human, can smell an airplane when I climb into it. But the sheep were all around the airplane.

There was a ewe with her lamb not ten feet from me on the boulder to the right! I dared not move, but could only turn my head. Then I realized that I had left my camera in the airplane. How foolish! I had even bragged a little that if I kept that camera with me at all times, someday I would get an outstanding picture. Most certainly, here was the opportunity, and I had blown it. There were sheep on both sides of me within very close range and I had no camera in my hand.

I chastised myself for my thoughtlessness, but there seemed to be nothing I could to about it. After a few minutes of turning my head without moving the rest of my body, I decided to see if I could possible make it to that plane and get the camera. I rolled off the rock to my left and put an arm and leg down to cushion my fall. I made it, although I landed in a somewhat cramped position. I had to raise my knees to get turned around because I was headed the wrong way. I made it around successfully without any disturbance and started trying to crawl to the plane on my belly. But after about ten feet, an old ewe about 30 feet away said "pfft," or something like that—a sound of warning without a doubt. I laid perfectly still, hoping she would forget about me and go on feeding, but she did not. She just said "pfft" again, and I looked around and every sheep in that pasture was looking directly toward my position. Then the old ewe just took off on a trot and every other sheep gathered around her into a rather tight bunch and took off. They ran over a small rise and soon were out of sight. I raised up and then saw some rams as well. Rams dot not generally mix with the ewes in summer, but at times they come together briefly. Had I waited and had the presence of mind to have my camera with me, the rams would probably have come close enough for some good pictures, too. When the rams saw the ewes leaving, they started off, too. They did not run, just turned and walked off, feeding as they went. I was once more alone with only my Cub. I cussed myself very good for my thoughtlessness, you can bet.

Except for the camera fiasco, everything else turned out all right. The gravity-testing scientist returned with his successful reading. Then as time went on, we got on up to the higher altitudes, and with very favorable weather and wind, clear up to the 14,000 foot level. So that part was fine, but I was still very sorry about missing those outstanding pictures of our wonderful Dall sheep.

THE GRAVITY TESTER 65

Gene Effler took this outstanding ram in the Wrangells in 1959. The longest horn is only 42 inches, but the B&C score is 183 pts.

Caves are common in sheep country. Sheep often use them—as do sheep hunters.

CHAPTER 7
NEANDERTHALS

Alaska had so much to offer—it was amazing. The myth still persisted somewhat that Alaska was a land of perpetual ice and snow, with wind and constant storms, and people were living in igloos—a very uncomfortable place to live. But, of course, it is nothing like that at all. I just sometimes wonder how the myth ever got started. Actually, Alaska has a very good climate. In summer it can and does get very hot and stay that way for a lengthy time. Of course there are cool periods, but they can still be comfortable times. If one just wears adequate clothing appropriate to the occasion, that is all it takes.

I have sweated so much on a hot day while hunting sheep that my clothing was completely soaked. Of course there is ice and perpetual snow with great glaciers and icefields present in the great mountains, but they are only in certain places. They add to the beauty of the great country. The scenery of these magnificent icefields is superb. They are an added bonus and are utilized by mountain climbers and scientific teams as well. I have taken many teams up into these glaciers and landed them there for their climb; then brought them back safely to the lower altitudes where there are roads and hotels and superb restaurants.

So, all in all, Alaska is a great place. The winters, of course, are very cold and last for a lengthy period of time, yet they have value as well. People have warm dwellings to live in and most of them have electricity. Cars are plugged in and can be operated when it is 40 below. The roads are well-plowed and mostly free of ice. Winter recreation has come a long way with the most famous dog races in the world. There are thousands of snow machines and people enjoy skiing and other outdoor sports. With adequate clothing and temperatures of only 10 or 20 below, outdoor activities are very much enjoyed in winter.

Of course, to those of us who had decided to become guides and hunters, the most enjoyable time of year is during the early fall hunting season. Then we can ply our trade of taking hunters out in quest of sheep or other big game. We can enjoy the outdoors in this great country of ours and live a superb life.

Usually, we guides had our own outfit and a certain "bailiwick," or area, chosen to hunt in; an area we became very well-acquainted with. Once in awhile we teamed up for a joint hunt. It just so happened that this is what took place one fall when the sheep season arrived. Ed Bilderback down on the coast had booked a hunter for coastal brown bear when the season would open on September first. His hunter wanted a goat and a sheep as well.

Ed had flown up to the interior with his hunter and got Harley King, an old friend, to fly them into the Tana River drainage—a large tributary that came in from the south to the Chitina River. From there, they would go goat hunting. At the same time, Harley had booked a sheep hunter and planned to take him to McCall Ridge and hunt sheep. Not knowing what these friends of mine were doing, I had also booked a hunter to hunt McCall Ridge.

This ridge, lying north of the Chitina River, is miles long and parallel to the river itself. It is rugged with several rimrocks on the south slope, but these can be easily gotten around on a climb. On top, it is reasonably easy going with smooth ridges and valleys. There were several bands of Dall sheep on this ridge—possibly more sheep than on any other single mountain system in the Wrangell Mountains; many sheep and large bunches of rams, many of them full curl and very fine trophies.

A sheep hunter with his trophy, around 1960.

This is where I wound up with my hunter, finding Harley there with his. He had gone over to the Tana River and picked up Ed and his hunter and brought them over as well. They had collected a small billy goat on their hunt. We all sat down and cooked some of the goat meat while we visited. A young billy or nanny goat is good to eat. However, an old billy is no good at all for human consumption. They get so tough and smell so bad they cannot be eaten at all.

We decided that we could all hunt the ridge, since there were a lot of sheep up there. We would stay together for our climb, then split up; each guide and hunter going his own way and taking however much time as was necessary to collect the trophies.

About halfway up the ridge we had discovered a large cave on previous hunts. This was the best place for a spike camp we had ever seen. It was roomy enough for all of us to sleep in without the need of a tent. The floor of the cave was dry sand and comfortable to sleep on without a mattress. The cave was just above a rim of rotten granite; we had cut steps in this rock to make it safe and fairly easy to scramble up there. Being just at the timberline, below the rim was some scraggly cottonwood, stunted spruce, and brush we called pucker brush. That meant we could have firewood. Just below the rim was a little spring with clear, cold water adequate for drinking purposes and coffee.

This cave had everything, and we had left cans of food and other items there on previous hunts. This time we would take along quite a bit of food, however, in case some of us needed to camp there for however long it might take to get a sheep. We packed up and climbed to the cave that afternoon. Generally, on sheep hunts we did not ask our clients to pack a load, but all three of these hunters wanted to pack something. So we all took small packs and arrived at the cave that evening. Then we gathered wood and water and had a good meal.

The next morning, after a breakfast of pancakes, bacon, eggs, and coffee, we got started up the mountain for our hunt. All of us had our packboards and haversacks, field glasses, knives, saws, whetstones, and other necessary stuff for a sheep hunt.

We arrived at the main ridge and there Ed stopped us. He said he would like to sneak up there and take a look over the ridge in case there were some sheep nearby. After a good look he carefully came back down and said, "Holy cats! There are a bunch of rams bedded down, just over the ridge, a large bunch of them. Plenty of fine rams for all if we can get them. Lets give it a try."

We were surprised at this statement, but paired up—each guide and hunter together—and assaulted the ridge like soldiers on a skirmish line. We peered over the top and there were the rams, many of them as Ed had told us. I found a very good one, whispered to my hunter which one it was, and told him to go ahead and shoot if he wanted. He wanted it all right and lined up his rifle and shot the sheep. At the same time the others shot and there was quite a scramble, but all three hunters got a good sheep. In all my years of hunting I never saw anything like that happen again.

Three full curl rams in one photo—a rare occurrence, to say the least.

When things settled down there were congratulations, posing and photos taken, and a lot of handshaking. Then we settled down for the work—the business of carefully removing the capes and cutting the meat up into pack-size proportions. After some lunch we loaded up everything and started back down to the cave. With all of us it was easy to pack everything.

After a good rest at the cave we decided that we were going to have a big feast. I am not sure the hunters knew just what we were going to do, nor how we would go about it, but they would find out in due time.

Sheep hunters with trophies from the Nadina River, 1955.

We climbed down the cliff face and spread out in both directions to find a good deal of firewood. We hauled all that up to the cave and brought up water. Then the preparations began. We cut two complete rib cages off the sheep. Fresh sheep ribs are superb. All sheep meat is very good, as I have described before; but the ribs, before they get a dry crust on them, are hard to beat anywhere.

The total preparation was going to take quite a lot of time. However, we had plenty of it since we had decided to stay at the cave one more night before going on down to base camp. Luckily, none of the hunters was on a time schedule that would not permit a little relaxation. There are many ways to prepare sheep ribs over an open fire, but our chosen way was a very primitive one, albeit a method we had often used before for sheep and caribou ribs. We drove two green sticks into the ground slantwise, so their top ends would be above the fire. Then we sharpened the sticks.

We started our fire, using non-resinous wood, and kept adding more as it burned down. After a time we had a good bed of coals. We told the hunters to help themselves to the candy bars and other trail food we had to tide them over until the feast was ready. When the fire was burned down so it suited us, we speared the rib cages on the pointed sticks with their lower ends near the fire. We had nothing to baste these ribs with, yet they are self-basting because, as they started to cook, the fat started melting and sliding down—finally dripping into the fire where it flamed up momentarily.

The lower portions of the ribs started to get black and it became necessary to adjust the sticks just right so they would not burn too much. Soon we had our feast ready. The lower portion would be well done, above that would be medium rare, then medium, then rare at the top portion. We were famished and started helping ourselves to it before it was really very done, all the time chattering and having a fine time.

We sat there and cut ribs off, holding them in our hands while we ate the meat and fat off them. Since much of the meat had turned black, our hands and faces turned black and greasy as well. But we kept right on and the stories flew, some of them probably not entirely true, but good stories nonetheless.

The hunters got into the act and liked the meat, but they did not go about it with as much gusto as we guides. All in all it turned out to be quite a feast. We ate it all before we were finally full and ready to relax on our sleeping bags. Finally, though, we were tired and ready to sleep.

Next morning we went down to base camp where there was plenty of water and we could get cleaned up good and prepare a complete meal—instead of just meat alone.

Then one of the hunters had some remarks about our feast the night before. He said, "You know, you guides were really something last night. Why, it took me all the way back to ancient history and the time of the cavemen. There is plenty of evidence that cavemen lived in caves. After they discovered how to make fire and weapons capable of killing game, they built fires at the mouths of their caves and cooked their meat just about the way you fellows did last night. Most probably they laughed and joked and bragged about their prowess as great hunters. In fact, I don't believe man has progressed as far as we may believe. Last night proved that we still have the caveman instinct, especially among you three!"

After that, for a long time, we were known as the Neanderthals.

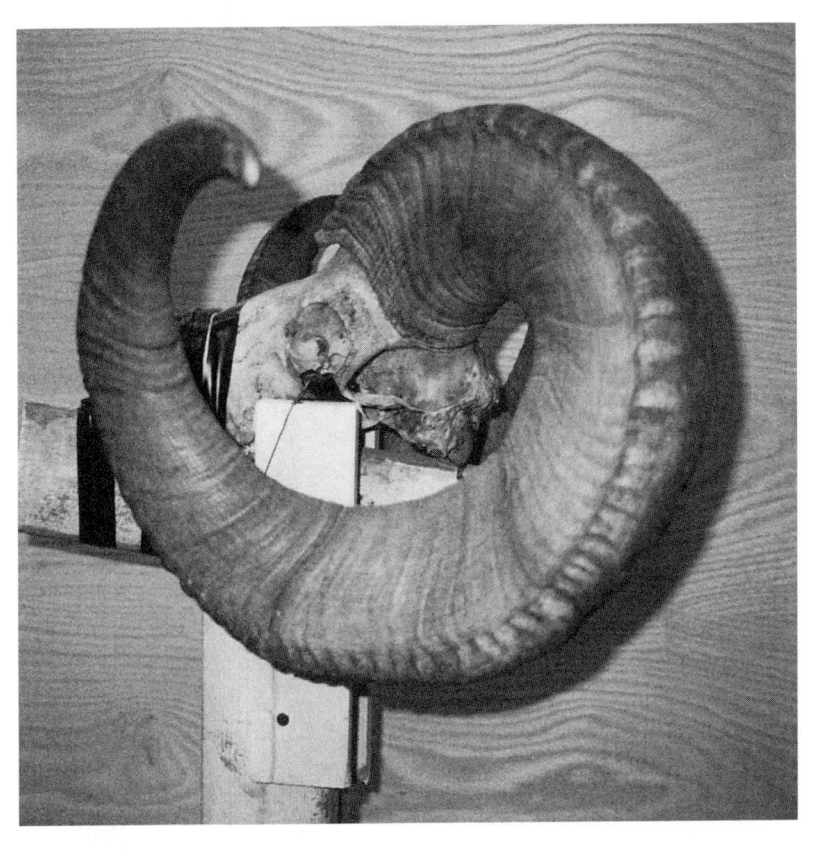

This set of sheep horns is 45 inches long and scores 176 B&C pts. It was picked up near the Nadina River in 1996—which shows that there are still a few huge sheep left out there for hunters who haven't given up on the big ones.

Jack Wilson, pilot, holding the World Record Dall sheep horns taken by Harry L. Swank, Jr., in 1961.

CHAPTER 8
THE WORLD RECORD DALL RAM

Many, many stories have been written about hunts for sheep, some of them very interesting, and some of them very boring. It is easily possible for an author to embellish the story to make it sound interesting, whether it really was or not. However, in the telling of this story, I want to write it exactly as it was.

The World Record Dall Ram was taken in 1961 by Harry L. Swank, Jr., a resident of Anchorage, Alaska, where he and his father had a sporting goods store. He was an experienced sheep hunter and a good sportsman. I had taken him on his first sheep hunt in 1958 and he had collected a very good trophy. Each year for the next two he had hunted again with me. On his third hunt he had not taken a ram at all, but had hunted for a full week with a pack on his back along with a friend. He had seen many sheep, had gotten close enough to them to look them over very well, yet not seeing anything he had really wanted, had not shot anything. I liked that. I had never really cared for hunters who had become game hogs and wanted to shoot something each year, even if it was not a very good trophy. Harry was a true sportsman and a man very easy to like. He was built very good—being tall, wide of shoulder, and with an athletic build. He could carry a terrific load on his back.

The ram we speak of here was a well-known ram. In 1959 I had flown up the Chitina Glacier and seen a very large ram and a smaller half curl ram on the high slopes above the glacier. From a distance in the air I had glassed them. The old ram seemed to be a very big one, though from such a great distance I could not tell a great deal about it.

I was able to land on a good gravel bar on the river and set up a spotting scope. They were very high and still very far away, yet it showed me something. The ram seemed to have good horns, not broken, but probably more than a full curl. It was hard to tell much more since there was nothing to compare him with. Had he been running with some other large rams I could have used them for comparison, but with only the small half curl around it could not be done. I remembered the ram, though, for the possibility of hunting him in the future.

Later on that year, since no one else had hunted the ram and wanting some time off from the heavy flying, I went after him myself. However, I only had two days off and it was not enough. There was cloud cover at the 5000 foot level on the mountain, although it was clear otherwise. I climbed high enough, hoping the clouds would clear off, but they never did and I had no luck with the hunt. It was good to be out in a beautiful setting in such a wonderful country, however, and I enjoyed it.

The old ram and his companion showed up at the same place on the mountain for two more years. This was not too unusual. Sheep more or less remain on the same range for their entire life. They also move on that range at certain times of the year to the same part, probably following the feed as they like it. So there they were at the same place each year and they were noticeable. It is a wonder that no other hunters went after the big one during such a long period of time except myself and my own hunters. Although there were many

THE WORLD RECORD DALL RAM 79

hunters by then, and a lot of them flying their own airplanes, it is likely that most hunters wanted a bunch of rams to hunt so they could compare sizes and sort them out. Just one ram alone could be risky to hunt. It just might be that he would elude the hunters and not be as easily found as a larger bunch. For whatever reason, so far as I know, no other hunters went after the ram during the period mentioned.

These two rams were photographed in 1990 on the same mountainside where the World Record Dall ram was taken. Both have massive horns.

In 1960 there was the old ram again, in the same place, at the same time as the previous year. This time I sent one of my guides after it. I had booked a hunter who was about 60 years of age. He wanted nothing less than a very large trophy. He claimed to be in very good health and could make the hunt all right—he said.

Alongside the great Chitina Glacier, about three miles up from the terminal moraine and the beginning of the large Chitina River, was a place we called the "Slot." Between the side moraine and the mountain to the north was a narrow little valley, nearly level. It had some spruce timber and some small cottonwoods and willows. We had been able to land an airplane there; then had improved the spot until we had a very decent landing strip, suitable for our Cessna aircraft. This was a wonderful spot for a base camp, having all it needed for a perfect campsite. There was plenty of firewood, open level space, and a small, clear stream that chuckled along for a water supply. It was a place we liked very much. I had always enjoyed this great wilderness we had and truly loved good campsites.

This is where I placed my guide Jim—a very good guide who was half Tlingit Indian—and the old hunter. It was to turn out that the hunter, although in good physical condition, had developed bad knees; yet believed he could make the hunt all right.

Jim and the hunter climbed the mountain early the first morning after Jim had produced a good breakfast. After a long climb the hunter's knees started to give out, yet he persisted and managed to get higher. Finally he could go no further, so Jim decided to let him have a long rest along with some lunch. After a couple hours Jim asked the hunter to try it again, and he did, but he just could not make it any further up the mountain. Jim told him to rest some more and he carefully climbed higher until, with extreme caution, he had gotten a good look at the old ram with his glasses. He was able to tell me later that it was by far the biggest ram he had ever seen. He then went back down to where the hunter was resting, hoping the old fellow could make the short distance on up to within stalking distance of the ram. It was not to be so. The hunter said he would go no further. He also declared that we had earned our fee and that he would not complain about it in any way. So, sadly enough, they eased back down the mountain and back to the base camp where they could wait for me to pick them up. That was the second year of the old ram—1960.

THE WORLD RECORD DALL RAM 81

In 1961, somewhat unbelievably, there the old ram and his young companion were once more in late July, right on the same range they had been in the two previous years. I had supposed the old ram probably died the previous winter since he was very old, yet there he was.

Harry Swank had contacted me and wanted to go sheep hunting again and I decided to send him after the old ram. We sat down and planned the hunt. Harry was going with a friend once more, but since I already had been up the mountain and knew the terrain quite well, Harry wanted me as guide. This I was glad to agree to. I attempted to arrange to take the time off from flying so I could do the job properly.

When the hunting season opened, we flew up to the "Slot" alongside Chitina Glacier. Then we packed up another three miles or so to a side glacier, appropriately named Ram Glacier. This was a mean little glacier, very rough and broken, and quite active as some glaciers are. We had no need to cross it, which would have been difficult. The ram we were after was on our side.

Here, at the spot I had chosen for their camp, was where I left them. I had more flying to do that evening and had to fly back to my base at Gulkana and get it done. I told Harry that I could be back very early the next morning so we could go hunting. He said he would wait for me, yet as so often happens in a bush pilot's life, it did not work out as I had planned. The people who were going on the charter were unavoidably delayed and I was forced to wait for them. Due to this, I did not get all the flying done until the next morning.

At the sheep camp Harry and his friend had arisen early. It was agreed between them that Harry would hunt the old ram and the friend would hunt other sheep we had seen, so he started out in their direction while Harry waited in the camp for my arrival. However, he became restless and since he was very ambitious, decided to do something, at any rate. So with a small pack on his back that included his spotting scope, and with his rifle crooked in his arm, he started walking up alongside Ram Glacier. By doing so he would get around a spur of the mountain and be able to glass the upper slopes, and possibly spot the rams from the different location. He had no intention of actually hunting.

On his right was the mean glacier with its side moraine of rubble piled high in a ridge alongside. On his left began the steep slope of the mountain. In between was a game trail between the two and easy going. Harry sauntered along, following the game trail. He suddenly heard a small rock or two come plink, plink, plinking down off the rubble. This is not an unusual sound alongside an active glacier, yet it caught his attention and he looked ahead and upward. There, up on top of the rubble, stood a three-quarter curl ram. Just ahead of Harry was a small bush, so he hunkered down behind that and it offered partial cover. He watched and the ram did not see him. Then a very great ram showed up on the rubble and stood alongside the smaller ram. Harry immediately figured this was the ram he had come after. Somehow, for reasons unknown, the rams had left their high pasture and come down here to the glacier. One can never tell just what an animal may do.

Harry admits that, at first, he got buck fever and wanted to start shooting; but he managed to control that urge, realizing that neither sheep was aware of his presence. So he waited.

After a short time, the rams started down off the rubble very carefully and they caused rock to slide ahead of them, which created noise, yet the rams eased their way on down. Finally, the great ram stood on the trail about 40 yards away from Harry, and he shot it. And that is how it came to be that a new World Record ram had been taken.

THE WORLD RECORD DALL RAM

The Harry L. Swank, Jr., ram. As of 1997, this ram still holds the World Record Dall sheep status. 189 6/8 Boone &Crockett points.

Harry was a product of chance. He had merely been in the right place at the right time to take the trophy. It had happened with no long climb up a high mountain. He was no more than one-half mile from his spike camp.

Harry went up to the old ram and was immediately amazed at the size of both the animal and the horns. With a small tape measure he measured the curl of one of the horns and it came to 49 inches. In the sheep hunting fraternity a ram with 40 inch horns is considered a fine trophy. With a 44 inch curl and reasonably large bases it can be entered in the Boone and Crockett Records according to their way of measuring a trophy. But here this great specimen had a 49 inch curl and very large bases. Harry knew that he probably had a new World Record, although it could not be measured according to the Boone and Crockett standards until a waiting period of 60 days to allow for normal shrinkage—as required with all trophies.

Harry carefully measured the ram as well and made notes. It was taller and longer than the usual Dall ram. He measured the girth of the neck as well to provide information for the taxidermist he would hire to make a mount of the sheep.

He caped it out as he knew how to do; then with a small saw, removed the upper skull and horns from the lower skull. Then he busied himself dressing and skinning out the carcass and cutting the meat into pack-size portions. Then, after loading up the horns and cape, he returned to camp. This had all been accomplished during the morning hours—a very short hunt.

At about noon I was finally able to reach the "Slot" and tie down my airplane. Then with a small pack, including my sleeping bag, I walked up the three miles or so to the spike camp—where I expected Harry would be waiting for me to guide him after the sheep.

Upon arrival, I found both hunters in camp. Harry's friend had stalked some sheep, but found the ram he was after had a horn broken off. He did not want it and had returned to camp. There I found Harry grinning at me, but I also noticed that his clothes were bloody and wondered what was going on. Then Harry zipped open his little mountain tent and rolled out those horns and I did a double take. I knew right off he had killed a new World Record.

We laughed and chortled and had a good time. But there was work still to be done. So with our packs, the three of us went up to the carcass of the ram and brought the meat down to camp. Then we loaded and divided the spike camp between the three of us and slowly made our way down to the "Slot." We loaded everything into the Cessna 180 and left that very good airstrip for the trip to Gulkana.

None of us had a camera along to record this great event, so we got no pictures of the great trophy until we were on the ramp at the airfield. Harry, a product of chance and a very happy man, had a very happy look on his face when his picture was taken.

None of us had a camera along to record this great event, so we got no pictures of the great trophy until we were on the ramp at the airfield. Harry, a product of chance and a very happy man, had a very happy look on his face when his picture was taken.

I am sorry to report that Harry Swank was killed in an aircraft accident in 1963. He had gotten the ram mounted, had won the Boone and Crockett Sagamore Hill Trophy for the greatest big game trophy for 1961, and the ram had been easily entered into the Records of North American Big Game as the new World Record. It is still the World Record as this is written more than 30 years since the event. It possibly will hold the World Record status for all time.

By counting the horn rings we determined the old ram was 14 years of age, older than most rams ever get. It is doubtful that he would have lived another season. The horns, after the 60 day waiting period, measured 48 and 5/8 inches for the one on the right and 47 and 7/8 on the left. The bases were 14 5/8 inches and 14 7/8 respectively—very, very big for a thinhorn sheep. Altogether, the total Boone and Crockett score was 189 and 6/8 inches, much larger than the number two Dall ram. It was, and is, an amazing trophy. The mounted head is now owned by Mrs. Harry Swank and the last I heard, it was on display at the Wild Game Museum on Fort Richardson Army Base at Anchorage, Alaska.

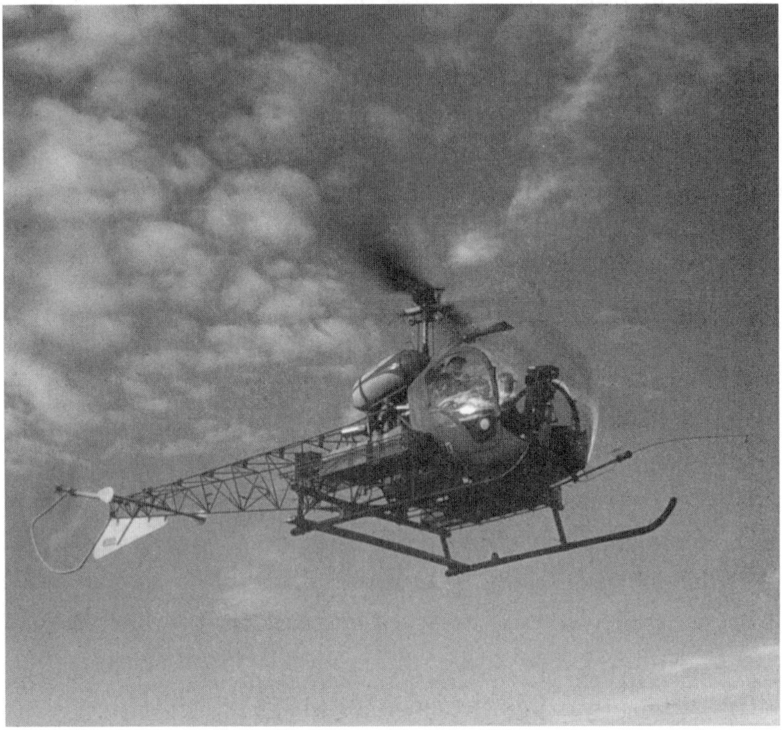

CHAPTER 9
HELICOPTERS

The Wrangell Mountains are known as the most highly mineralized part of Alaska. Great deposits of copper ore were discovered here around the turn of the century. It is said that an old chief—Nikolai— of the Ahtna Indian tribe showed some prospectors large bodies of ore after they had agreed to give him a large pack train of supplies for services rendered. This old chief was a good businessman. Prospecting continued and more ore was found, much more, a lot of it being very high grade. There was even float of very high grade found on slides in the region.

Business interests in New York were attracted, money was invested, and Kennicott Copper Company came into being as a result. Mines were opened in the mountains and a big ore mill was built. A railroad was built up the canyons past the treacherous glaciers of the Copper River from Cordova at tidewater; a means of transportation for the ore which was shipped to the West Coast and milled into pure copper. By 1911 operations were begun and the largest copper mine in the world came into operation. Every day a trainload of ore went to Cordova and was shipped to the West Coast for smelting. Several hundred miners moved into the area to do the necessary work, and the supply town of McCarthy was built down below the mill and became a supply and recreation town for the miners.

This great operation kept running until the autumn of 1938. By that time millions of tons of ore had been shipped. But the ore supply—as seen at the present time—was dwindling. And the price of labor was going up and the price of copper was down. The great operation shut down for the time being and many of the people left for other horizons. Some stayed with the hope that the mines would open again. Yet they never did reopen the mines. With World War II looming on the horizon, the United States had decided Alaska was too vulnerable from invasion from Japan and that it would be dangerous for the country to continue mining operations in such a remote location. It was also decided that copper in other parts of the world would be safer to mine and that there would be an adequate supply of copper from these other, safer places to conduct the war to its successful conclusion.

When the great and terrible war finally ended, Alaska took on a whole new look. Japan had tried to invade, but had botched the job; and the world, including Alaska, was free to once more pursue peaceful subjects. Thousands of American servicemen had come to Alaska during the war and had seen what a wonderful country it was. Therefore, the myth that Alaska was a perpetual land of snow and ice was forever dispelled. They had found that the climate in Alaska was not only just bearable, but that it could be comfortable to live in and was a very pleasant, attractive country. The coastal climate was very wet. Yet the temperatures were mild and there was seldom very much bitter cold weather. The interior had a fine climate, though there were very cold winters. These winters were livable, not unlike the winters in some of our northern states. And the summers were wonderful, with long hours of daylight and hot weather. It was an ideal climate and, therefore, there was the beginnings of a much larger population.

Alaska had many, many resources—both renewable and nonrenewable. These resources were looked at with the idea of future development. One thing that got started in a big way was mineral exploration. The largest mining companies in the world had risk capital to spend for the purpose of locating more minerals. A great effort was started to find and catalog bodies of ore that would be worthwhile to mine. The Wrangell Mountains, known to be the most highly mineralized area of the territory, were explored very carefully.

Horses were used to transport geologists before the developments in helicopters made them indispensable.

Teams of geologists went into the wilderness and climbed the mountains to prospect for mineralized areas. In the Wrangell Mountains copper was the mineral most sought for. Even though the great Kennicott mines were closed forever, there was still copper—a great deal of it—to be found, and eventually mined.

The first large efforts at mineral exploration after the war ended were conducted without the use of helicopters. Although helicopters had been flown during the war and were coming along rapidly, they were not, at first, suitable for exploration due to their inability to operate at high altitudes. They could not take the geologists to the heights needed to find the ore deposits. Exploration teams were flown to the wilderness, but the men had to *climb* the mountains, and had to move from one location to another with the use of horses. There was no other way to get it done.

In the 1950s helicopters began coming on for mineral exploration. The newer models could reach the altitudes desired, so a change was made, and they were starting to be used extensively for exploration purposes.

This all started at the time that I was available to get into the game of doing extensive flying for these companies. I had arrived at the right place, at the right time—it turned out.

The exploration teams usually arrived in Alaska during the month of May and were then flown to a wilderness area to conduct their work. They continued on during the summer months until sometime in August. At this time, early snow in the high mountains would signal the time to stop operations. The teams would then be flown back out and would not be seen again until the next year.

Taking care of these teams created a lot of flying, and was lucrative for me and other operators who happened to get started with them. An exploration team generally consisted of two or three geologists, a party chief, and a cook. They all had to be flown to a wilderness airstrip; their camp gear and food had to be flown out as well. During the term of their stay they needed to be supplied with all their food and necessities. Then, when operations were ended in August, they all had to be flown back in again. This was very good business for me and I welcomed It. The exploration teams left the country just as the hunting season was beginning and there was only a small overlap of these two enterprises.

HELICOPTERS 91

The flying for these exploration teams was very lucrative; I sometimes had two or three parties at the same time during the summer months. The small helicopters they used brought me business, too. They had to have a lot of fuel to fly the geologists around and that had to be flown out as well. The helicopters needed considerable maintenance to keep them going as well, which meant flying mechanics and parts back and forth. All in all I was doing very well with these companies, and their pay was good.

Three rams relax on their rocky perch, where no creature can harass them—except men in aircraft.

Suddenly, I found myself perched on the horns of a dilemma. The helicopters were scaring the sheep, which inhabited many of the mountains they concentrated on. I have mentioned before how "buzzing" sheep with a fixed-wing airplane would scare them out of the country. Well, the helicopters were much, much worse at scaring them. The sound of a helicopter coming absolutely terrorized the sheep. They would panic badly and run as far and fast as they could.

Sheep are very sure-footed animals and in their rugged, natural habitat they can go anywhere they wish to, and do it safely enough. Yet they never hurried when going about their country. They moved slowly, but surely, and seldom went faster than a walk in difficult terrain. But a helicopter approaching would put them in a panic, and they would take off running as fast as they could move. Just the sound of the rotor blades in the distance would start them moving. If the chopper came too close they thought themselves to be in great danger. They would run off as fast as they could go and there was bound to be accidents, even for these great, sure-footed animals. I have flown over herds of sheep and seen blood on their sides where they had fallen and slid down on the sharp rocks. I have seen them carrying a leg that was broken, and I have seen their dead bodies down on rock slides below the cliffs where they have fallen to their death.

This devastation—a very sad situation—was the result of progress, and I realized there was absolutely nothing I could do about it. I had gloried in getting the business of flying these exploration parties to their locations on the one hand; on the other hand I hated all of this. It was hard to see the sheep herds harassed like this. Again, there seemed to be nothing I could do about it.

Naturalists have reported that sheep, if harassed a great deal and often, will eventually leave their range for another one and not again return to that same country for a long time. They might eventually return very slowly, but no one knew how long it might take. I saw this occur on Nikolai Mountain where there roamed a large herd of sheep. They just disappeared and were seen no more. In time we believed they went up the west fork of the Nizina River and joined the herd up there. This was in extremely rough country, hard to hunt, and very remote. The helicopters did not work in that particular area very much so it was left alone. There was not a great deal of mineralization up the west fork anyway. That is where they stayed and I do not know if they have ever returned.

A group of ewes and lambs running from perceived danger (a photographer). Understandably, aircraft can drive sheep into a frenzy to escape, with disastrous results.

The helicopter pilots did not want to scare the sheep, but they had their jobs to think of and had to perform for their company. One pilot said that he always tried to circle at least once before he came within sight of the sheep to give them a chance to move away from the area he was taking his passengers. Of course that helped some, yet just the sound of the rotor blades was enough to put the sheep in terror.

This exploration went on for years, through the 1970s. I went along with it all, hating it, yet still glad to have the business of furnishing air support. There was just no way to prevent these things from happening.

Outlaw guides were out to take as many animals as possible, because numbers meant money to them.

CHAPTER 10
OUTLAW GUIDES

In 1959 Alaska was admitted as the 49th State of the Union and was no longer a Territory. By 1960 our new Legislature and Governor had a new guide law in place. It then became necessary for us guides to get registered with the state. To become a registered guide a person needed to have been a resident for a period of at least five years, and have no known game violations on record. He, or she, had to have a good knowledge of the country where the hunting and guiding would take place and must have a very good knowledge of the animals that would be hunted, along with other requirements.

There was a written examination and an oral one. If a person did know the country very well and the animals that inhabited it, as well as the game regulations, there was no big problem to pass the guide examination. A novice would usually flunk the exams, but a person who really wanted to become a guide and had the ability to become one could pass it with ease. Many of us applied and became registered Alaska Big Game Guides.

We took an oath to uphold the laws of the State of Alaska and to report any and all game violations that we might become aware of. By far, most of the new guides fully intended to abide by these laws since we wanted to keep on being good citizens. But there were a few who had no intention of doing this. Therefore, we acquired some who would become outlaw guides.

Alaska has some large game animals; transporting meat out of the field was costly, but mandatory.

Another one of the guide laws stated that nonresident hunters must hunt Dall sheep or grizzly bear with a registered guide. This law assured business for all the guides. Hunts were booked up in advance, sometimes many months in fact, before the hunt would begin. Some of the guides over-booked hunts and took on as many hunters as they could possibly take on for trophy hunts—especially for sheep, which was the most popular of all the trophy big game animals in Alaska.

They then established a good set up, found a good place to do their hunting, and hired adequate help to conduct their business. They became game hogs and attempted to take any and all trophy animals available.

To be successful in these enterprises the outlaw guides violated every game law written. The object was to take all the trophy animals available and the devil take the hindmost. They freely hunted the same day they were airborne. The "Same Day Airborne" law, based on the "fair chase" principle, meant that a hunter must land his airplane, establish a camp, then wait until the next day before he could begin hunting. Certain small aircraft, mostly the Super Cub, could land in many places in wilderness Alaska. It was sometimes possible to land the airplane, get out, and shoot a trophy animal right there before it could get away. Such was the reason for the law.

These guides violated every other game law written when it became necessary—in their minds—to hasten the finish and get the desired trophy. They became like men in our Old West in the nineteenth century whose object was to "get rich quick and get out."

They often harassed game with aircraft. It was not unusual for an airplane to drive sheep up the slope and over a rim right into the guns of hunters already placed in position for shooting. They killed any kind of big game animal and let it lay in a good place to use the carcass for bear bait. Even if bear season was not open yet, that made absolutely no difference at all. They made many violations and found they could get away with it with impunity. They often used two-way radios so the pilot in the airplane could tell the guide on the ground where a trophy was so they could stalk right up to it. They left meat in the field and violated the wanton waste law. It is written that a hunter must take all the edible portion of the meat from a harvested animal for human consumption. The outlaw guides took little meat—sometimes just a small amount to use as camp meat. Packing in meat takes time and employees for the packing, and that meant money had to be spent. Therefore, most of the meat was left in the field to rot.

The game department was helpless to stop and control all these violations. Alaska is too vast and big to be patrolled adequately. Funds in the treasury of our new state were very low. About all the money to be had for game management and enforcement came from the sale of licenses to hunters, and these funds did not stretch very far. So the violations went on, and though the state tried to stop it all, they were not very successful.

It was very hard to get a conviction for these violations, sometimes even with good evidence that one or more violations had occurred. A good lawyer could usually get the culprit set free with no penalty. There was a way to get convictions, but it was a costly, time-consuming process. An agent would be planted in the hunting camp of the suspected guide. This meant that the agent had to be unknown in Alaskan circles. The agent needed an Outside address and phone number and had to get booked for an extended hunt with the guide. Then, as a hunter, the agent could use a small tape recorder concealed on his person to record all conversations. He would take copious notes and observe all activities—legal and illegal—and use a camera wherever possible. By this means the state did get some convictions, yet not very many. The penalty was stiff when a conviction was made. The state confiscated the guide's guns and his airplane, then imposed a stiff fine and a jail sentence.

While all this was going on the legitimate guides, of which there became many after statehood, went on plodding along and hunting without breaking the regulations. They made a pretty fair living, yet none of them ever got rich. Some of the outlaw guides, however, went right on, unhampered in our great wilderness country, and made quite a pile.

When the hunting seasons for sheep, moose, caribou, and other animals closed near the end of September each year, many of the guides went to coastal areas and hunted brown bear. The brown is actually the same animal as the interior grizzly, yet they get somewhat larger since good food is more readily available. There are many, many streams draining into costal waters in which Pacific salmon spawn, creating an overabundance for bear and other creatures. Alaska has very many brown bear in the coastal regions, or at least in some of the coastal regions. Remember, Alaska has several thousand miles of coastline.

Many of the guides, both legitimate and illegitimate, used Super Cubs for transportation on the Alaska Peninsula—a good place to hunt brown bear. The pilot/guides could land on the beach and hunt at will in this country where there were few trees. The country was open enough to easily spot animals—including bears.

*Eleven days of fair-chase hunting paid off for this hunter. Some **would-be** hunters were willing to pay outlaw guides to get a bear by any means.*

The outlaw guides went right on with their nefarious activities. Although they sometimes established camps, they often hunted the same day they were airborne. It is possible to drive bear to a certain degree with an airplane. While the bear is not afraid of most anything in the country, they are leery of the terrifying airplanes and will try to run away from them. Thus, the pilot could put his hunter and guide in a certain place and, sometimes, drive a bear right to them. There were even cases of the guides doing the hunting themselves. A very rich man could book up a hunt, come to Alaska and buy a hunting license, then be flown out to a luxurious wilderness lodge. There he could live high on the hog with private room and bath, the best steaks to eat, and all the booze he wanted. Then, for an exorbitant fee, their guide would go out and hunt the somewhat dangerous animal, get a good specimen for the hunter, then bring back the hide. The hunter could then go back Outside with his trophy and brag to his friends about what a great hunter he was, without having gone through any risk whatsoever in the process. He had not been required to undergo the rigors of camp life. He had avoided the wet coastal weather in a place where terrific wind blows. He had lived a life of luxury while his guide illegally got him a bear.

There were even cases of guides killing brown bear, then peddling the hides outside to rich clients, but there was not a great deal of this. It is too risky smuggling hides Outside.

During their heyday the outlaw guides operated in all areas of Alaska. We were never aware of some of their activities, since we remained in our own part of the great country and did not necessarily know what was going on in other parts of the state.

In time the outlaw guides did diminish in the state, but this was not because they were convicted of game violations. Many of them were never caught. Attrition was what did it. Some of them merely retired. Some who had made their pile moved Outside and invested their money in some other enterprise. Some of them grew old and died. At least one of them suffered a tragic accident . . .

In our part of Alaska a young guide started coming every hunting season. He outfitted at Tolsona Lake, where there is a little dirt airstrip alongside the lake near the lodge. He became very well known in the country and was well liked. He was a handsome man, had a fine personality, and there was always laughter in his actions. People thought a lot of him and he was known as Slim.

Dall sheep will come down below timberline in early spring to get at the new grass—easy prey for outlaw guides who ignored closed seasons.

But Slim was an outlaw guide. Some people knew this fact for sure, others suspected it, but no one could do anything about it. He was different than some of them in that he was not trying to make his pile quickly and then get out. He was, for the most part, a loner. He did most of his flying and guiding himself and hired very little help. His object was to be very successful as a guide, get all the trophies his hunters ever desired, and not to take forever getting it done. Therefore, when the need arose he would break any game regulation in the book to get the job done. Having found out that he could—if he was very careful not to get caught—guarantee his hunts; he charged a higher fee for his services.

One year he booked a hunter that wanted a mixed bag of trophies. Sheep, moose, grizzly bear, and caribou were all desired by this hunter. This would create quite an extended hunt. They got outfitted at Tolsona and then departed from the lake for the Chugach Mountains to the south. Slim did not tell anyone just where they were going since he liked to be secretive as to where his base camp would be. This would lessen the chance of a game warden dropping in and messing things up. Actually they went to the Hallet River, which drains into Klutina Lake near its headwaters. Slim was a good outfitter and had already set up a good camp before the arrival of his hunter.

They decided to first concentrate on sheep hunting, since there was a mountain nearby which contained some very good rams. However, these sheep had already been hunted by someone else and been spooked up into very high country. So Slim decided to wait a few days on the sheep hunting and let them quiet down and return to their normal pastures. Meanwhile, they could do something else.

They decided to go moose hunting. They cruised the country from the air looking for a trophy bull moose in just the right sort of location. It was not too long until they found just what they wanted.

On a ridge above the very large, glacial Tazlina Lake at about the four thousand foot level they saw a large trophy-size moose. He was feeding in the pucker brush above the timberline. It was possible to fly over this animal very low so Slim could see the value of the antlers as a trophy. Moose, unlike sheep, are not afraid of aircraft flying quite low over them and generally will not move at all, unless buzzed very closely. This moose turned out to be a very good trophy, just what the hunter desired. Slim looked around and found he could land right there on the ridge above the moose. After landing, they walked down to within rifle range of the moose and the hunter shot it.

Moose are generally not afraid of airplanes; they can be approached quite closely from the air and on the ground.

After congratulations and the necessary pictures they removed the antlers and the upper skull from the remainder of the skull. Then the antlers were tied on the wing struts of the airplane. They left all the meat in the field to rot. Here they had violated at least two regulations. They not only had hunted the same day they were airborne, having jumped out of the airplane and shot a big game animal, but they had left every bit of that good moose meat in the field to rot. But there was a purpose here. The moose would become ripe within a few days and might attract a grizzly bear. Therefore, one reason it was left was to create bear bait.

It worked too. In a few days they flew over the moose kill and there was a large boar grizzly feeding on the kill. Now, a grizzly, upon discovering a kill—whether it is fresh or rotten—will claim it for his very own. Grizzlies are known as the "King of the forest," and will stay there at the kill as long as it takes to consume it. It must have been a great thing for that bear to be able to claim so much free food. The bear will defend his kill from all comers, and nothing on the North American continent can run him away from a kill except a larger, more ferocious grizzly. Not even a human. Grizzlies are not necessarily afraid of humans. It is true that if you meet a grizzly on the trail, he will stand up and look at you with his poor eyesight. His great head will move back and forth to get your scent—grizzlies have a keen nose. Upon getting the human scent he will then usually turn and amble off. They just do not like the human presence and will generally avoid encounters with humans whenever possible. But afraid of them? I don't think so. It may be that bears have developed an instinct to avoid humans since men generally carry a rifle and can deal death from a distance. I cannot really answer that for sure.

Anyway, Slim and the hunter flew over and, upon seeing the bear on the kill, landed the airplane in the same spot they had landed for the moose; then walked down the mountain to get closer to the bear.

When they were within easy rifle range they could not see the bear, since the high brush obscured it. Although they had been able to take the moose from this position, the moose had been much taller. Then Slim did a very foolish thing. He might have said something like this: "You stay here and have your rifle ready to shoot that bear. I will go down there and dog him out." Just like that! That is exactly what he did.

As I have mentioned, a bear will guard his kill from all comers and do it with violence if necessary. I believe everybody knows that. To this day, no one knows why Slim went down there to "dog" the bear out so the hunter could see it and get a good shot.

Now the story has been told that a bear, from a standing start, can outrun a racehorse for a short distance. I have no idea whether this fact has been proven since man has had horses in America. I do know, from the experience of having once been charged by a bear, that they can, indeed, run terribly fast.

Moose, caribou, sheep, and buffalo horns taken by Jack Wilson's guiding operation. A mixed bag like this is possible for fair chase hunters in Alaska, but there were guides who wanted to do it the easy way.

Slim was successful in his endeavor to "dog" the bear out all right. Instead of moving away from the kill as it might have been thought to do—so it could be seen, it did nothing of the kind. It came straight toward Slim.

The hunter above, prepared to shoot the bear when he moved into the open, had no chance to do so. Things happened so fast, neither he nor Slim had a chance to use their rifles. Although the hunter did kill the bear when things quieted down a bit, it was too late. Slim was dead.

It must have taken the hunter quite some time to recover from the shock of what happened. But then, when he did recover, he began to realize what a terrible fix he was in.

Here he was, in the wilds of Alaska, with no idea of where he was nor where to go from there. Slim had never told the man where they were so he had absolutely no idea where he was. Actually, it was only about 15 miles to a major highway from his position, but he did not know that.

In his dilemma he happened to walk near Slim's airplane and he heard some noise that sounded like radio static. Upon closer observation he found that Slim, in his hurry to get out of the airplane, had left the master switch on as well as the radio. Although the hunter had no knowledge of how to fly an airplane nor operate any of the switches and levers in the cockpit, he did know how to use a radio. So he put out a distress call. It so happened that Slim had been tuned into the local FAA station, possibly to get a weather forecast or other information, and they answered the call. As well as he could, the hunter explained his trouble. He said he was on a ridge above a very big lake. The radio operator believed he knew about where that might be and an airplane was dispatched to go have a look. The hunter was located, then a helicopter with a state trooper on board went up there. They rescued the hunter and brought in Slim's body.

The hunter was cited for several game violations, even that of hunting bear before the season had opened on these animals. He was considered as much of a violator as had been his guide. The hunter admitted everything as being true and would have probably been convicted and fined very heavily, with a possible jail sentence as well. However, the sergeant of the state troopers recommended leniency since he claimed it was his opinion the hunter had already suffered enough. So the hunter was let off with a reprimand and they confiscated his rifle and removed his hunting privileges for a number of years.

Thus came the tragic end of a very good, but dishonest man.

Dall rams have a strict social hierarchy and can often be observed rubbing horns—as these rams are doing—or butting horns to establish dominance.

CHAPTER 11
THE BATTERING RAMS

The two words "Battering Ram" stem from rams, both domestic and wild, that have a habit of backing off, then running and leaping together and battering their heads and horns. Even some domestic sheep have horns quite similar to those of a wild ram—which are the ones most likely to engage in this "sport," if it can be called that.

The dictionary states: "Battering Ram–A military engine anciently used to beat down the walls of besieged places and consisting of a large beam encased in iron and somewhat resembling the head of a ram."

For a long while I wanted to observe this business of wild rams butting their heads and horns together. One time, I looked down from high above some rams as I flew by and had a glimpse of two rams engaged in this pastime. However, I wanted to see it from the ground. It was quite a few years until the time finally came one fine August day in 1966.

Since 1959 1 had often done the flying in the Wrangell Mountains for Hal Waugh, Alaska's number one master guide. It had been a very good relationship and meant several hours of flying time for me each year. Hal had a camp in the Alaska Range at a place called

Post Lake, from which a stream drains down to the South Fork of the Kuskokwim River. There, he and his guides could take Dall sheep, moose, and grizzlies at times. Yet Hal wanted to "crop" his hunting country and did not want to take very many rams each year, giving the younger rams a chance to grow to full curl status. Another reason was that the Post Lake rams, although beautiful specimens, did not have horns as large as some of the rams in my country in the Wrangells.

I had a lot of sheep and the Wrangells at that time had never been hunted very heavily. So it would be possible to let Hal and his guides take a few more rams in my part of the country without hurting the ram population one bit. The story of our adventures in Alaska is well documented in the book, "Fair Chase with Alaskan Guides," Alaska Northwest Publishing Co., 1972. It is a fine book written by Hal Waugh and Charles J. Keim—Professor of Journalism at the University of Alaska, Fairbanks. Mr. Keim, or Chuck, as we called him, was a very good big game guide in his own right and collaborated with Hal as a guide for a number of years.

Hal and his crew took several beautiful rams from my part of Alaska over the years; our relationship and admiration for each other grew as time went on. Hal was a true "fair chase" guide. He did not need to have me spot sheep for him. All I had to do was say there were a number of good rams in a certain area and that was good enough for Hal. He and his hired guides would do the rest. They would scout the country and find the rams, without the assistance of an aircraft to do the spotting for them.

In 1965 Hal had a hunter named Doctor Bob Broadbent, a young physician from Reno. He had hunted with Hal on previous hunts for moose and grizzly bears. Bob was a fine fellow and very well liked. He had gotten his "Grand Slam" on sheep, meaning that he had taken a Dall sheep, a Stone, a Rocky Mountain bighorn, and a

THE BATTERING RAMS 111

John Liska took this ram from the Wrangells in 1963. 174 3/8 pts.

desert bighorn. However, his Dall sheep had not been a very great trophy and he wanted a better one. He asked Hal if he could get him a good, big Dall, and Hal had said he would talk to me and see what we could manage for a hunt.

I knew of a place we called the "Devil's Hole," where there was a good bunch of large rams that we had never hunted. I suggested taking them there. I explained to Hal that it was a tough spot to hunt because I could never figure out a way to get into this great basin from the lower side. I told him the only known access was from the upper side. This meant I would land them on Nikolai Mt. at the 6000 foot level, then they would have to scale a ridge and go down the other side into a great basin where the rams were. He asked why that was. I told him that from the lower side on West

Fork—a tributary of the Nizina River—there were high cliffs that prevented access. Also, it would be dangerous to go up the right side of the creek and attempt to cross the West Fork Glacier since it was a mean glacier and quite active. Therefore, the only access I knew of would be from the upper ridge above the basin.

They established a base camp on Nikolai Mountain after I flew them up there. The next morning they scaled the ridge above and went down into that great basin and located the rams. They found what they wanted and Bob took a fine ram which would score 170 6/8 in the Boone and Crockett Record Book.

Hal was getting along in years and it was hard for him to get out of that great basin and up over the high ridge with a pack of sheep on his back. But Bob was young, strong, and willing. He carried the greatest amount of the weight so they made it out of there with the horns, cape, and all the meat Bob could pack. Hall then recuperated at their base camp on top of the mountain until I got in there and flew them back to civilization.

Hal told me that there were at least a dozen rams down there, most of them full curl, and he was not even sure they had taken the best one of all. They had taken the first ram Bob had seen and wanted for his trophy.

I remembered all that and knew I was going to somehow find a way to get into that fine hunting spot from the lower side, no matter how long it might take.

The next summer, 1966, a couple young fellows showed up at my office in July. I asked them what they were up to at that time of year. They said they were just bumming around until hunting season began and knew they would be working for me as assistant guides. They had quit their summer jobs and were just hanging around until the season opened.

That gave me an idea, so I told them that if they wanted two or three days work I would hand them each a double-bitted axe and put them to use. They said sure thing to that and we got ready to go.

I took one of the men with me in the Super Cub and we managed to make one successful landing near the mouth of the West Fork of the Nizina River on a gravel bar. We then removed driftwood, dug out rocks, filled the holes with sand, and generally improved it until it was a very passable airstrip for a Super Cub. Then I went back and brought in the other man. With a camp set up we were all ready to begin our task in the morning.

We crossed the stream next morning and assaulted the alder brush and small spruce trees, cutting a trail up to those cliffs which prevented passage to the country above. When we reached the base of the cliff we cut along it, looking for a place to somehow climb up there. Soon we found what we wanted. The cliff suddenly ended, and another one started beyond it. Yet there was a gap 10 or 12 feet wide that looked climbable. We trimmed the brush out of this passage, then, using the dull sides of our double bitted axes, cut steps in the dirt and climbed right on up until we stood above the rimrocks. It looked like we had it made! After more brush trimming we proceeded right on up until we were above most of the brush—in the open tundra where it was easy going. Satisfied, we went back down to our camp, packed it all up, and flew on back to Gulkana Airfield. We had accomplished our purpose and, of course, did not tell anyone else what we had done. I wanted to keep this place for my own use—at least until the word got out that there was a way to get into that great basin above.

I booked up a hunter who wanted a better than average Dall trophy and when hunting season arrived we went up to the West Fork, again with a Super Cub. I flew in an assistant guide, Brady, who would go along as packer. Brady was coming along nicely as an assistant guide. I was about ready to turn him loose and let him guide a hunter on his own. He was also about eligible to take the tests and become a registered guide on his own part.

The hunter said he would be glad to pack along with Brady and I. So we loaded up what we needed to make a spike camp part of the way up the mountain and packed up through the gap we had prepared between the cliffs. We went on up into the tundra to a level spot where we erected our little spike camp. We had sleeping bags, a small mountain tent for the hunter, and waterproof ponchos for Brady and me. We also had a little Primus stove and a small can of fuel for heating water and cooking. We were well fixed for a stay on the mountain.

We then began our trek on into the great basin and found it to be easy going and a fine place to hunt. There were hills and ridges, but there were little valleys in between and it was easy to proceed without our quarry seeing us. Since we were entirely new to this country, we proceeded with caution.

Being in the lead I looked behind me, and there was Brady and the hunter squatted down on their haunches to lower their profile. I asked Brady what he was doing. He said they had spotted a ram feeding on ahead and had hunkered down to keep from being seen. Brady wondered if perhaps the big bunch of rams was there as well. I said they might be, or, as sometimes happens, the ram they had seen might be off by himself. I suggested that he take the hunter and go see. I knew Brady would handle the job all right. So they cautiously proceeded onward, staying out of sight of the ram.

I sat down on a boulder to wait for them. After awhile I became restless and decided to climb the small hill above me and look over the top. It seems as if one must always see what is on the other side of a hill. So I went up there, but with caution, since I did not want

THE BATTERING RAMS 115

to silhouette myself on the ridge. I crawled up there and peeked over the top. There, perhaps 200 yards away, were the rams; at least a dozen of them—and big ones at that. Some were lying down, facing all points of the compass, and two or three of them were up feeding. I took my field glasses and looked them over good. There were at least two of them that were very good trophies.

"... after recuperating from the shock of their second battering exercise, those two rams calmly started feeding alongside each other, as if nothing had happened."

Suddenly, two of the largest rams faced each other and both struck forward with a front foot. Then, suddenly, they ran together, their front feet came off the ground and their hind feet remained on the ground and pushed forward. Their heads and horns came together violently and it knocked them both silly. Yet they got right back up again and I noticed that one of them had a bloody nose. I thought if that had happened to me I would have much more than just a bloody nose, I would have a fractured skull. Then, those rams backed off and did it again! Wow! What a sight to see. I was tickled to death.

This had been one of the greatest shows I had ever seen in my life. Then, after recuperating from the shock of their second battering exercise, those two rams calmly started feeding alongside each other, as if nothing had happened.

I eased back down from my position on top of the ridge; went back to sit once more on the boulder; and waited for Brady and the hunter, Don, to return. After a brief wait, I saw them coming. There had been no shot fired so I knew they had not found a suitable ram for the hunter.

Brady told me it had just been a three-quarter curl ram feeding alone and they had backed off without their presence becoming known.

So I said, "Well, lets go hunting, I know where the rams are." Then I explained about the rams being just beyond the hill at a distance of about 200 hundred yards and that there were at least two very fine trophies there. The next thing on the agenda was for us to make our stalk. I also briefly mentioned the two big rams battering their heads together a couple times.

Then we carefully ascended the small hill and peeked over the top, the hunter with his rifle ready and myself with my own rifle to back him up. I whispered to Don which ram was the best of all and told him to go ahead and shoot and be ready to shoot again if the first shot did not get the ram. The rest was easy, since the hunter was calm enough to aim properly. He got the ram in a vital spot the first shot and it fell dead. The other rams then got together in a tight bunch and started off away from us. We had what we had come after and it had not been a tough hunt at all.

Next came the congratulations and some pictures. Then, I reached in my pack and produced three miniature, two-ounce bottles of scotch I had brought along. I knew this hunter liked a drink or two before supper and I sometimes brought along the small bottles so we could have a little drink while the congratulations were being made.

Then the work began, but even this was enjoyable in such a beautiful setting. We caped the ram out, then butchered it properly, and cut the meat into pack-size proportions. With the hunter packing a load as well as Brady and me, it would work fine to get all the meat as well as the horns and cape in one trip.

We slowly made out way back down to our spike camp and remained overnight, since it was getting quite late.

The ram's horns measured a full 44 inches on the curl and were not broomed at all. Although the bases were rather small and it would not make the record book, it was a truly beautiful trophy. That was the happy ending of our hunt, yet there was a final unhappy ending in later years. The hunter, Don, had the head mounted by his taxidermist and proudly hung it in the office. Later, thieves broke into the office and stole the head. Don was never able to recover it.

Lew Anderton, guide for the Duke during the 1930s hunt.

CHAPTER 12
A SHEEP HUNT WITH THE DUKE

This is the story of a sheep hunt made many years before my time; a hunt made in the 1930s when I was still a small boy on a cattle ranch in Colorado. It is a good story and worthy of being told as it was told to me long ago in about 1955.

The story was told to me by Lew Anderton, an old time horse guide and outfitter in Alaska. Lew had been a horse man in Montana and had continued on with horses after coming to Alaska. He had settled in at a small log cabin village in Southcentral Alaska named Chisana. Chisana was the way it was spelled on the map, but it is pronounced "Shushana." Obviously an Indian name, no one seems to know why it is misspelled on the map, but pronounced differently. That is just the way it happens to be.

Chisana is a log cabin village in the Nutzotin Mountains, located between the White River drainage—which enters the Yukon Territory, and the Nabesna drainage—which flows north to the larger Tanana River. Chisana is a picturesque place in a beautiful setting below the timberline at about the 3500 foot level. The white spruce timber in the area made fine logs for building the village—which was situated on the Chisana River. It came into being in 1913 when there was a small gold rush to that area on Bonanza Creek, just a few miles to the north.

The Chisana River flowed past the log cabin village as a braided glacial stream and furnished adequate food for the Anderton horses. Although the winters were very cold, snowfall was not very heavy. The horses could paw down to a legume—called peavine, and another plant—called wolfberry, and do quite well in winter. Lew supplemented their diet with grain flown in by the early mail planes, which came more or less on a weekly basis.

Lew was contacted through correspondence by an English nobleman—a Duke, no less—who wanted to come to Alaska and hunt Dall sheep and grizzly bear. This Duke had hunted extensively in Africa and India—so he wrote. The negotiations for the sheep and grizzly hunt started about a year before the hunt could begin since mail via ship across the Atlantic Ocean was, of course, rather slow in those days. Yet, in time, the negotiations were completed and Lew agreed to take him on the extensive hunt.

The hunt would start from the mining town of McCarthy on the Kennicott River, about five miles from the great copper mill at Kennicott. The Copper River and Northwestern Railroad extended from Cordova, from tidewater to these interior mines. A daily ore train left Kennicott for the coastal town where the ore was loaded on freighters and sailed south to the West Coast, where it was smelted into copper. The train returned to McCarthy, pulling a passenger car or two for movement of people to and from the area.

Lew would meet his hunter at McCarthy and, when the time came, went from Chisana over Chitistone pass via the "goat trail"—which had been hacked out by miners through the pass. The route then took them down the Chitistone River to the Nizina River; then on to McCarthy.

At McCarthy they did the final outfitting for the hunt and waited for the arrival of the Duke. Lew had a large pack train and a couple of wranglers with him to help things along. Upon arrival of the Duke they prepared to go with the pack train over to the Chitina River, then up the river to the terminus of the Chitina Glacier where the sheep hunt would begin. This country they were traveling is the same country I would take over in the 1950s, about 20 years later.

It must have been an interesting, enjoyable trip up the river 40 or so miles to the glacier terminus. In later years my travels over this same route would, of course, be made by aircraft. They arrived at the glacier terminus and camped near the Martin Harrais cabin nearby; an old cabin with a metal roof and in a beautiful spruce-covered locality.

They loose-herded the horses on Bryson Bar nearby, where in later times we would land our aircraft. They set up a very elaborate, comfortable base camp at this location. The Duke had his own large tent containing not only his bunk, but also a canvas folding bathtub and a reclining chair. He was accompanied by a young valet who took care of his every need, including helping the Duke dress in the morning. The valet had his own small tent pitched nearby.

Along with all the elaborate gear the Duke had brought along were two folding canvas chairs, very well built. Lew did not know just what these chairs were for, but brought them along anyway.

Lew had always been an early riser. He was usually the first one up each morning to get the coffee pot on the fire and start preparing breakfast, but he found the valet up ahead of him. He would have the coffee pot on and be heating water for his master's tea and his bath. When this was ready the valet would go to the Duke's tent, wake him, and hand him a cup of tea. Then he would prepare the bath. Upon completion of that, the Duke would recline in his chair while the valet shaved him, laid out clean clothing, and helped him dress—at which time the Duke would be ready for his day.

After setting up a comfortable base camp and allowing a couple days for the Duke to rest up from the long horseback ride, it was time to begin the sheep hunt.

Now, the mountains on the upper Chitina River are very steep. Instead of flattening out on top as many of the mountains do that harbor sheep, these go steadily up to the ice cap above the 8,000 foot level—where it is glaciated and always winter. There are little ridges and valleys, however, and it is possible to remain in cover when climbing to prevent being seen by the rams.

Lew and his wranglers had located sheep from below, on the river bar, and knew where to find them on the mountain where they would be feeding or resting. They would have no problem locating a trophy ram after getting up there.

Lew found out what one of the folding chairs was for. The valet tied it on his packboard along with a short-handled shovel. When it came time to rest on the long climb, he would use the shovel to smooth out a level spot for the chair. Then his master could sit there at ease and rest until the climb began again.

The wrangler went ahead, scouted out the sheep, and reported this to Lew—who got up in position with the Duke and prepared for the stalk to get a good trophy ram. He directed the Duke to come along with him and the Duke motioned for the valet to bring his rifle, which the valet had carried up there; but Lew told the Duke to leave the valet where he was and to carry his own rifle. The Duke was somewhat miffed at an ordinary American giving him orders and made a mild protest. Then Lew got very stern and informed him that they had come up there to get a Dall sheep and that was just what they were going to do; he was the guide, and therefore the boss; and the Duke would do exactly as he was told and be quiet about it as well.

They began their stalk then. When they got almost to the top of the ridge where they could look over and see the rams, Lew made the Duke get down on his belly and crawl up there. The Duke turned out to be a true hunter and had no trouble dispatching the sheep with one well-placed shot. The hunt was all over and we can assume the Duke was a well-pleased man.

I acquired the folding arm chairs. Lew told me they had left them in the cabin on the Martin Harrais mining claim at the head of the river. In 1957 I obtained permission from Martin's widow, Margaret, to use the cabin for a base camp and found the chairs on a shelf above the bunks in the cabin. Margaret Harrais was the Magistrate in Valdez, Alaska, at the time; but was killed during the tidal wave, or tsunami, which followed the devastating Alaska earthquake on March 27, 1964. My wife Bonnie made little cushions for the seats, and for years we used them for furniture in our house. I still have one of them out in my wood shop.

I assume the Duke and his valet returned to the British Isles, happy with their extended sheep hunt and the grizzly hunt—which was not related to me by that old time guide, Lew Anderton.

photo by Lavena Pierce

A Rocky Mountain goat in his summer coat. Winter pelage produces the long mane, pantalooned forelegs, and pointed beard.

CHAPTER 13
GOAT HUNT

The Rocky Mountain Goat, Oreamnos americanus americanus, had never been my bag—so far as guiding goes. I was familiar with the animal; both in the interior, where I hunted the white Dall sheep, and in the coastal area to the south. I knew that goats liked the damp coastal areas as well as the dry interior. I also knew they were related more to antelope than to goats.

Goats seem to be well named as Rocky Mountain goats since they range down through the Rockies from Alaska through Canada and into the contiguous 48 States.

Although I had never guided a goat hunter, I had hunted goats a couple times. When very new to Alaska, I had gone hunting with a couple friends out of Cordova, Alaska, one autumn. We had gone up the Copper River a few miles above the old railroad bridge, then climbed a mountain festooned with beautiful alpine tundra and had found numerous goats.

We killed two goats and one of the fellows had the misfortune to wound one. Although it was bleeding freely and was very easy to track, we could not get it. That goat simply went up into such rugged terrain that we could not follow—it became too dangerous to try to do so. We had to abandon our search.

After I got married, I once had flown up the Chitina River with my new bride Bonnie, along with her little dog. While she waited in an old trapper's cabin I had climbed a little way and gotten a nice young billy. I saved the horns from this animal and had a throw rug made of the skin. The meat was delicious. But I was to learn that the meat from an old billy is not good to eat. It is stringy, tough, and strongly flavored.

Most of the trophy goats taken by hunters came from British Columbia, followed by Alaska next. Trophies have been taken from several of our northwestern states. Their horns are black and seldom exceed eleven or twelve inches in length. Since both sexes have horns it is rather difficult to determine sex without being reasonably close to the animal. Only the males reach record book size; the bases of their horns being larger than the bases on the nannies. That is why a hunter must be fairly close to determine sex. Goats have long, shaggy hair which reaches down to their knees and pointed beards. They are very pretty animals. At times it has seemed to me that they resemble an old man with a pointed goatee and "high water" pants.

Goats' natural habitat seems to be in even more rugged territory than that of sheep. They seem to like country where there are rimrocks terraced clear up to the skyline along with large boulder patches. At times it looks like there is not enough feed to sustain any kind of animal where they roam, yet the goat seems to thrive on country where the vegetation is very scarce.

When hunting goats a person needs to evaluate the country before he shoots at a goat. They live and thrive in such tough terrain that it is possible to shoot one where getting to the animal is impossible.

I had never conducted a guided goat hunt since coming to Alaska, but had concentrated on sheep and other big game animals. Other guides conducted goat hunts, however, and it was my usual habit to just turn prospective goat hunters over to other guides more experienced in evaluating trophy-class animals. Goats were not sought after with the same fervency as sheep. Yet there always comes a time when a person can do something different.

"Goats' natural habitat seems to be in even more rugged territory than that of sheep."

In the autumn of 1977 I was sitting in my office relaxing and enjoying myself. It had been a good year, but now all the mineral exploration parties, mountain climbers, scientific teams, and most of the hunters were gone from our part of Alaska. Early October was upon us and it was Indian summer. The days were calm and sunny with beautiful autumn colors running riot and the nights were getting nippy. It was a nice time to relax, catch up on some reading, and rehash some of the things we had done during the summer. I was enjoying this respite from the frantic, heavy work of the summer season.

The door to my office opened and a young man stepped in, a very tall man with wide shoulders and a big grin on his face. I offered him a seat and a cup of coffee, then waited to see what was on his mind. He started talking about goats and that he would like to hire a guide to get a goat, since he had never hunted these animals before. He also mentioned he had plenty of time for a goat hunt. He had been a construction foreman on a road job for the last several months, but the work had ended for the season. He went on to say that he was not especially after a record book trophy, but just wanted a respectable goat. He wanted three things: a nice set of horns, a hide to have tanned for a rug, and the meat to eat.

I had been about ready to recommend another guide who was very reliable and experienced in hunting goats, but this sounded like something I could probably do myself—even though I was not an experienced goat guide. I knew where there were numerous goats in rugged, but huntable, country. It would be great to get out one more time for the season, enjoy the outdoors, and do something I would like to do. Experienced as a guide or not, this seemingly nice young man just wanted a respectable goat. I could certainly produce one if the hunter could shoot straight. So we resumed talking about it.

We hashed everything out and started getting prepared for a hunt. The hunter, whose name was Ed, had a fine personality and was very eager and helpful. He had a good outfit, a rifle he liked, good outdoor clothing, and a good down-filled sleeping bag for the cold nights to come. We got all outfitted that day and I used a prepared food list to buy our food for the hunt. A prepared list is something every outfitter should have. It can be very embarrassing, and sometimes uncomfortable, if something like the salt or coffee or something else vital is forgotten.

The next day we were all set for our trip and flew up the Chitina River, opposite a very rugged part of McCall Ridge, and landed on a smooth sand bar. We taxied over to a little cove near some large spruce timber in a very nice spot. There was plenty of fresh water there and a lot of firewood was handy. As we flew in we could see goats above us on the mountain, but did not fly close to them and possibly alarm them. We did not need, nor want, to look at them closely from the air. We could get up there and have a close look at them right from the ground when the time came.

Any sheep guide worth his salt could certainly get a hunter a respectable goat. Two of Jack's sheep hunters from 1962.

We busied ourselves making a good camp at this ideal spot. Ed was good at it and seemed to enjoy it as I always did. I was beginning to like this tall, good-natured man. We made a fire ring from some rocks, built a fire, set up a little grill for cooking, then put on the coffeepot. We now had a very comfortable camp and there was still enough daylight to do something else.

We went out on the bar where we could get a good view of the mountain and set up a spotting scope. Then we focused it on the goats above and brought them close enough to see much better. There were numerous goats up there, mostly scattered out in singles or pairs. Goats are not gregarious in the same sense sheep are and do not bunch up so much. That can sometimes be an advantage when hunting. If you should spook a goat and it gets away, you will not necessarily alarm other goats and can continue to hunt.

The scope showed goats at all levels of the mountain, from about 1000 feet above us on up to the top of the mountain. They were scattered about. We could see nannies with kids, which we would not want, and other goats of either sex scattered around at different levels amongst the big boulders and on the rims. It was nice to see that much from our position down on the gravel bar. It looked like a very good place to hunt.

Back at camp we prepared a good meal and spent our leisure time talking about previous hunts we had been on; then retired to our warm sleeping bags early so we could get an early start in the morning.

Shortly after daylight I had the fire going and the coffeepot on the grill, then stepped out on the bar for one more look through the spotting scope. We had left it out there, covered by an old jacket to keep the dew off.

The goats had merely moved around some, but there they were, showing plainly through the scope—some even visible with the naked eye. There were a couple of them not more than 1000 feet above us, I judged. I took a good look to remember where the first two were, as well as others which ranged on up higher. We were about ready to go.

After a good breakfast we went on our way, each of us with a small pack on our backs. I took the usual small tools as I always did when hunting sheep. There was a small saw for removing horns from the skull, extra knife, sharpening stone, and some small nylon twine for whatever was needed. Ed had said he would be willing to pack something and I liked that. He had only his raincoat on his packboard, but would be prepared to pack a load back down the mountain if the hunt was successful.

We got up through the heavy spruce timber, then started up through the high brush. When we got up there where it began to thin out the rest would merely be a very steep climb. I went leisurely enough, but soon found that Ed was lagging behind me, so I slowed my pace to stay back with him. Although I was quite a few years his senior, I could see that he could not keep up with me. Apparently, he was not in very good shape. I had thought he would be able to go right along with me, but he probably had spent several months just riding around in a pickup—going from one job sight to another and just not had enough exercise to keep in shape. It really did not matter at all since the climb looked like it might not be too lengthy for our purpose. We had plenty of time.

We got up there above the first rimrock and were walking around great boulders with scattered brush and small scraggly trees, mostly cottonwoods. I told Ed I would go on ahead and do some scouting, both to find a good route for us to take as well as try to spot some goats. I knew we were getting fairly close to the ones we had seen from down on the bar. Ed, with sweat showing through his shirt even in the balmy, but somewhat cool, October weather, was agreeable to that. I knew he would soon enough catch up with me.

I wound up around numerous boulders, got up there, and presently came to a small gorge that was uncrossable—a break down through the rimrock. This was really rugged country, one such as no animal but a goat would call home. Then I saw a goat on the other side of the little gorge, just standing there on a very narrow ledge facing me; but he did not see me. I was hunkered down with only the top of my head over a big boulder and had a good look at him.

This goat was a small billy, as I could see that the bases of his horns were quite large. It looked like his horns might go nine inches in length, not a large trophy by any means, just a young goat—yet a respectable enough animal. I had a long look at this magnificent animal and was amazed at the narrowness of the small ledge he was standing on at his ease.

There was no feed there and I had no idea just what his purpose was. But there you can see that I really did not know much about goats at all. He probably had a reason for being where he was.

I backed off and went down a small distance out of sight of the goat, which was only about fifty yards distant. I waited for Ed, as I could see him slowly moving up my way.

After Ed had a small time to sit and get his breath I told him about the goat and the narrow ledge he was standing on. I mentioned that it would be an easy shot, but if he shot, the goat would fall off that ledge, and it was quite a lengthy drop to a steep rock slide below. There was danger of a horn—or even both of them—getting broken if he fell off that ledge.

I then pointed out that we had two more options. One would be to spook the goat back the way he had come to a more favorable place to take him. The danger of shooting near him to spook him back was the nature of the terrain around us. It was very rugged there with big boulders piled one on top of the other. There were also the small trees and pucker brush growing around to obscure the view. There was a chance that if we spooked the goat back he would never be seen again as he went up the mountain.

The other option was to forget this certain goat, climb up higher, and find one in a more suitable spot; so I mentioned that to Ed.

Ed thought about it for awhile, but then said, "I really don't want to climb any higher if we can avoid it, though I could do it if necessary. I am inclined to shoot that goat where he is and take a chance of it getting a broken horn. The fall will probably damage him somewhat, but I believe I will take the chance."

This area of the Chitina River drainage where the goat hunt occured still has a good goat population.

So be it, if that is what he wanted. So I directed him up to where we could see over the last boulder. There we could see the goat standing on that little ledge. I knew I would not want to be out on a ledge that narrow, yet I knew this was not something unusual for a goat. It is hard to imagine the kind of country these nimble, surefooted animals can do well in if you have never had a chance to see them in their natural place on a very rugged mountain.

Ed carefully got his rifle in position, took steady aim at the goat, and placed his bullet right in the front of the chest. The goat humped up and then did just what I expected—he fell off that ledge. Down, down he went and hit the steep rock slide below. It bounced and went end over end, then slid on downward creating a minor rock slide, finally stopping on the steep slope. From up above we could not tell what the damage to the body might be, it was too far down below us.

We went back down the way we had come, down below the rimrock and turned left to parallel it until we reached the area below the goat; then started the climb back up. Since it was very steep, Ed slowed down again, but I went on ahead and found an easy way on upward. I came to a small draw and found a trickle of cold, clear water running down on the rocks and followed this small valley up toward the goat.

I came to a small mossy flat where I could see the goat above on the slide and waited there for Ed. He came along presently and we climbed the slide, grasped the rear legs of the goat, and pulled it on down to the little flat spot. Then we looked for damage and found the horns were all right. The hide on the backbone had split its full length, from the shoulder almost to the rump. The meat was exposed and some of the backstrap had departed from the backbone. It showed no other visible damage than that, but we would have to skin it to find out the extent of the damage from that long fall. It turned out there was no great damage. The slide had been so steep the body had not hit as hard as it would have on level ground.

After congratulating Ed on the clean shot he had made I commented on the fact that two of his desires would be fact. He would have some nice horns and some meat, even if the hide was ruined. But Ed thought differently. He wondered if perhaps a good taxidermist might be able to sew that hide back up again and make it as if there had been no damage at all. I thought it was possible and worth a try at least, so we started skinning it carefully. Ed said he wanted the hoofs and all, so I looked at them. I noticed that the hoofs on a goat are larger than those on a sheep. I seemed to compare a goat with a sheep in every way possible, yet there is really no comparison between the two animals—except that both the Dall sheep and the Mountain goat are white and about the same size. There is no other comparison between the two animals whatsoever.

We got it all skinned out, butchered up with the meat in pack-size proportions, and removed the horns. The meat did not look too bad and the body did not seem to be bruised as much as I thought it would have been. I divided the load into two packs about evenly and lashed them on our packboards; then we were ready to go downward, back to our base camp.

It was never comfortable packing downhill. Every step jolted me and seemed to hurt every muscle in my body. Yet Ed did not seem to notice it and started right on out ahead of me. Here I had a man who was a real heller at going downhill, even though he could not go uphill very well. He seemed to just saunter along as if he had nothing at all on his back!

We came to a sloping rock where I stopped for a rest. I sat down in a comfortable position, glad for the respite. Ed sat down on a boulder and waited for me. I recovered enough in awhile to sit up and load my pipe. Ed got up, came over to my pack, loosened the ropes, took part of my load, and added it to his. The larger load would not bother him at all—it was great having a client like this. Here he was paying me for the hunt, yet he was doing most of the work cheerfully!

It was much easier going now and we were soon at the camp for a good rest. The day was not over yet and there was plenty of time to break camp, then fly on back to my base at Gulkana. This hunt had gone very quickly and also been very successful. It had been a very enjoyable, if rather quick, trip; my one and only guided goat hunt.

J. M. Gerrish, nicknamed the "Boomerang" man because he made boomerangs for a living.

CHAPTER 14
THE RAM THAT BATTERED

In all my active years as a bush pilot and guide in our great state, formerly territory, of Alaska, I liked guiding for the great Dall sheep the best. Each year I spent time, as well as effort, guiding trophy hunters to these great specimens and enjoyed it all. I was the guide for Harry Swank, Jr., who killed the largest one of all in the autumn of 1961. This ram became the World Record and remains so today, 30 years after the event. During the years that went by, my hunters took many more trophy rams of record.

We had learned early on that Dall sheep reach full curl status at about eight years of age; also, that rams do not enjoy any great life span. About twelve years, or possibly one or two more years, is all they live. They might perish during a hard winter after getting old. Or they might get weak due to poor teeth at that time; and other factors probably shorten their life. We knew, then, that if we just killed full curl rams that we were not going to hurt the herds at all. The herd strength would remain constant. Younger rams would keep the herd strength up by taking care of the ewes during the fall rutting season, new lambs would be borne each year, and the herd would go on as strong as ever. We could kill the older full curl rams without any danger of harming the resource. This was satisfying.

So each year, during the hunting season, I took time off from an otherwise busy flying schedule and guided a few sheep hunters. I could have made just as much money by flying charters—which was a good business. I guided for sheep because I liked and enjoyed it. I learned a lot about sheep, knew where the big ones were, and the success rate was extremely good.

In winter, of course, we forgot all about sheep. They were still there, up on their mountains where the wind blew the snow off to expose food for them. We would see them from the distance as we flew past, whether on charter or wolf hunts or whatever we were doing. I had always wanted to take a sheep during the winter, since they grow a beautiful, long coat of hair—as could be seen if we flew close enough to them. Of course, I could not do that since the season was closed. It was just a wishful thought.

In 1960 and 1961 I had a good flying job. A big mining exploration company from Oregon had shown up in 1960 and set up camp at a pretty good airstrip in the remote Wrangell Mountains. They would use gasoline-powered helicopters for their exploration efforts and hired me to furnish them with full fixed-wing air support. I had contacted Jim Magoffin of Interior Airways in Fairbanks to bring a C-46 cargo plane down and fly some of their equipment, as well as the fuel for the helicopters, out to their airstrip. Then I kept them in groceries and other supplies and flew their executives in—then back out to Anchorage when they were ready to leave. It was a good job and, as it turned out, lasted all winter as well—something unusual with mining companies.

During that first summer—1960—they flew magnetometers around with helicopters and indicated they were locating ore that way. I had no knowledge of such things and did not care greatly anyway. I was merely interested in my own part of the operation. They claimed they had located a great deposit of Bornite (Copper ore) within a 6,000 foot high mountain with a rather round top. Then, they used seismic instruments they had flown up there and further verified the thought that they had located a great, minable body of ore. They staked out many mining claims on top of this local mountain. Their plan was to drill for this ore the coming season.

I had found I could land on that 6,000 foot mountain, although it was rather tricky. I had landed there with one of their geologists several times during the summer.

When winter approached, the boss of the mining operation informed me that they were going to remain there all winter to guard their claims. That suited me fine, since it would give me a winter flying job. Thus, with a C-46 load of lumber, plywood, and stove oil, they constructed some pretty fair, winter-insulated tent frames and were prepared to stay. They would leave a skeleton crew there: a geologist for party chief, a young man as flunky, and an old cook.

The boss then informed me that he would guard those claims very well all winter. He did not want them to be " jumped" during the winter. Therefore, he said he wanted me to fly that party chief up there at least once every two weeks so he could check each claim stake on top of that mountain. I told him that would hardly be necessary. I was adept at tracking from the air. By hunting wolves and coyotes I had gotten so I could track almost any animal larger than a squirrel expertly from the air. I told him I could merely fly over the mountain any time they wanted and I could certainly tell if there had been any human activity up there by the tracks they would obviously make. He informed me, rather curtly, that he would have an actual check of those claim stakes at least once every two weeks during the winter; and if I did not want the job he would find someone who did. So I told him I would do it all right, depending on snow and weather conditions; and that the only aircraft I would use would be the Piper Super Cub equipped with skis, not the larger, all metal Cessna aircraft. He okayed that part. I knew it was going to be a tough job. I also knew, if I should damage a Cessna up there, I would be in trouble. However, the fabric-covered Super Cub, if damaged, could be repaired right on the spot—at least good enough to get it flown back down off the mountain.

So that winter the party chief, who we called Bernie, and I would fly up there when weather permitted. Then with his snowshoes and clipboard containing his claim maps, he would snowshoe off and check each and every one of the claim stakes while I waited for him in the freezing wind. It was a little job I did not like, yet it formed a part of the living I was making.

In March the weather warmed up and it began to thaw. Bernie called me on the radio and said to bring the Super Cub on up; he wanted to check those claims at least one more time. I had already told him that when spring breakup came, I would not be able to fly up there and land on slushy snow. For that last trip I loaded the Cub with their groceries and flew out to their airstrip.

It was only a fifteen minute flight from the airstrip up to that 6,000 foot mountain so we went on up for a look. It did not look good at all. There had been a big wind a few days previously and great drifts had formed, like ocean swells several feet apart. It was going to be a tough landing. I flew around and finally picked what I thought might be the best spot and set it down to the roughest landing I had ever made. We slammed into those drifts, which were as hard as stone, and caromed off them. I was certain the landing gear would break. It was complicated somewhat by the snow in between the drifts, which was soft and wet from starting to melt.

Somehow the Cub survived that landing with no damages—a great relief to me.

Bernie got out with his snowshoes and clipboard and started off toward his stakes. He would hardly need the snowshoes on that hard snow, but took them anyway. I walked around over the top of that mountain looking for a better spot for takeoff. What I found was not too encouraging. There just were no good spots. Finally, I positioned the Cub above what I thought was the best place for a downhill takeoff and waited for Bernie.

When Bernie arrived, I said, "Looks like this is an impossible situation. There is no way I am going to get you out of here in that plane. It is just too rough and we will wipe out a landing gear sure as hell. I want you to walk down to that saddle below us—the saddle that goes over toward Nikolai Creek. I noticed on the way up that the snow is pretty good in that saddle. I can pick you up there with no problem."

Bernie didn't like that. He did not like it at all. He did not want to walk down off that mountain. I didn't blame him, but finally talked him into it anyway. I said, "Perhaps if I am solo, I can jump off one of these big drifts and stay airborne without breaking something. Lets hope so anyway. It's our only chance."

With that finally agreed upon, I started out. The Cub slammed over a couple drifts, which shook me up pretty bad and caused worry, but then it did leap off the next drift and almost made it. Yet it settled back down and the heals of the skis hit another one. It jumped again and that time it stayed airborne. I Looked with relief out both sides and was happy to see my landing gear apparently still intact.

I flew on down to the airstrip for a better inspection of the gear and found it all right. I then informed the other men that we had a little trouble and told them where I would be landing to pick up Bernie. Thus, they would know where we were in case we had further trouble.

I went back up to the saddle and landed, finding that it was a good spot. Then I looked up and there was Bernie, just a speck on the horizon, coming down and almost to the steepest part. It looked fine to me. Then I saw something else.

Below Bernie and to his left was a cliff outcrop, not a real big one, but a cliff, nevertheless, with a good overhang. Under that cliff was a herd of Dall rams lying there in the protection the cliff offered from the big winds. Somehow I had missed seeing these rams on our trip to the top, but there they were.

I grinned when I saw them. Bernie was going to come right down past the end of that cliff and would pass quite close to them. It would be a surprise to both him and the rams, but I did not worry. Dall rams are not belligerent and would merely run out and climb the mountain when they saw him. It would surprise Bernie too, I knew. Bernie would get a very close look at some wild rams at least—something few humans ever get the chance to do.

Rams do not fight humans nor predators. Practically their only defense is the ability to climb faster and more surefooted than any human and almost any predator. Wolves do get them at times we know, but often the rams can just out-climb them and out-distance them up an extremely steep mountain. Rams have great horns, but they are no good as weapons. Naturalists have marveled at this, knowing that the curled horns, which do not jut out forward or any other direction, are actually not good as weapons at all.

Rams do joust with each other, but not with their horns—except as extra weight. They will butt heads with each other often, and not necessarily during the rutting season either. They just like to butt heads. I had watched them on summer climbs as I went up a mountain to see how my big rams were doing and noticing what I would have for my hunters when the season opened. From a concealed position I would watch them at this play—if it could be called that. A couple rams would square off, then, as if at a signal, they would

THE RAM THAT BATTERED 143

rush toward each other with heads lowered. They would leap and hit in midair with a terrific, loud impact. It would be great enough to knock them off their feet, stun them, and bloody their noses. Then they would recover and likely as not do it again. They might keep it up for some time or else just go to feeding side by side again. No one seems to know why they butt heads like this. I saw evidence of it on trophy rams we killed; more than once I saw that a big ram's nose had been broken at some time, probably from this head butting.

I have read that ewes would do the same thing at times, but never have observed it.

"That biggest ram of all saw Bernie—suddenly only about ten feet away—and he stood up and charged."

I was an interested watcher as Bernie started around the edge of the cliff. There was a little swale there, a place where water had washed out a ditch around the end of the cliff. Bernie started down through that little swale. It was slick and icy there from the snow beginning to melt and Bernie started to slide. He "ran" with the slide, not wanting to sit down on his butt and get it wet. He noticed some sand below the cliff and turned and ran out on that sand to get stopped—and ran right into those rams!

As I have said before, rams are not belligerent at all, but this was too much. Any animal, when cornered, will fight for its own life—rams included. That biggest ram of all saw Bernie—suddenly only about ten feet away—and he stood up and charged. Bernie saw what was coming and managed to step back a bit. But the ram—head lowered—came right at him, leaped, and knocked him right off that sand onto the steep, snowy slope below!

From the great distance below Bernie I did not see all the action plainly. But suddenly, there was Bernie lying down in the snow and the rams bunched up above him and starting to climb that mountain—their only true defense. I did know a ram had knocked Bernie down there; however, I was very afraid he might be hurt badly. I started up there as fast as I could climb. But then I saw Bernie get up, stagger around a bit, then go to gathering up his cap and snowshoes. He looked around for awhile, then slowly started back down the mountain. I climbed to meet him and, when arriving, asked if he was okay. He said he thought so, but he was very shook up and nervous. I took his snowshoes and got him down to the airplane and got him loaded.

We flew on down to the airstrip, then got Bernie down to the tent houses and looked him over with his shirt off. He seemed to be all right, just shook up from what had happened, but not really hurt at all.

Bernie was then able to tell us what had actually taken place. When he ran around the end of that cliff and suddenly found himself staring right in the face of the biggest ram, he had instinctively stepped back a pace—which had helped some; however, he said what had saved him from injury was his snowshoes. He had them together and was holding them with his left hand, his wrist run through the bindings. Thus, he inadvertently had the snowshoes positioned the same as an old warrior would have used a shield. The ram, when he leaped, hit those snowshoes instead of hitting Bernie directly. The impact was therefore spread out and not necessarily damaging, just very surprising. Bernie had went off down into the snow with his breath knocked out somewhat, but not really hurt at all. I considered this a very lucky thing.

Then it was time to laugh. Since Bernie was not actually hurt I considered it a very funny incident, and the others thought so, too. Bernie, however, did not laugh.

After that, Bernie was rather standoffish to me. Though he stayed for awhile until he was relieved by another party chief, he was always rather cool to me. I suspected that he believed I had set him up for that whole incident, which, of course, I had not done at all. Perhaps it was partly because I had laughed so much and said, "Bernie, you are the only human, living or dead, that has ever been attacked by a Dall Ram!"

Above: Jack's moose camp near Mt. Drum. Below: "Requim to Moose Camp" painting by Gail Niebrugge.

CHAPTER 15
MOOSE AT THEIR BEST

In all my active years in my wondrous Alaska, I was a bush pilot first and foremost. And it is natural for a bush pilot to fly low and use terrain features for accurate navigation. This gives the pilot a wonderful opportunity to observe the great game herds that pass by below.

Mine had always been an insatiable curiosity about big game animals. I wondered how they lived, what they did, how they reproduced, and how they fought—with each other or with some member of another species. All these questions were, in part, answered by flying low over the game itself. Many other questions in my mind remain unanswered and will remain so. Often I flew charter for the Department of Fish and Game. On these flights, I carried a game biologist to count or observe the moose, caribou, grizzlies, or whatever it was the man was interested in at the time. These flights gave me an excellent opportunity to observe the game and their antics. We pried into their private lives shamelessly.

We saw many antics in the world of big game—some comic, some tragic. We once saw wolves successfully waylay a couple caribou. And we saw coyotes unsuccessfully and comically try to waylay some rabbits. One summer we saw three wolves harassing a big grizzly bear just for the hell of it—or so it seemed. They were just biting him in the butt as he tried to run away; then they would nimbly dodge away when he whirled on them. We watched as some wolves caught and killed a large trophy bull moose. All these things and many more passed beneath our wings on charter flights over the years.

Jack Wilson with one of his successful moose hunters on the slopes of Mt. Drum.

Moose became high on my list. I wanted to see just how they did everything in their lives, not just the reproductive cycle itself. The bulls and cows would take care of that in time. I wanted to see how they worked up to it—the preliminaries.

Moose are not ungainly animals as some writers have mentioned. To me they are lordly and very nimble for their size. The largest member of the deer family, a bull moose stands higher at the shoulder than a horse. They can trot very rapidly and cover a lot of ground very quickly through brush and timber almost too thick for a man to pass through.

MOOSE AT THEIR BEST 149

Among other things that I became interested in was the rut, or mating season, and how they formed harems of cows; how they went about fighting for the privilege of keeping a harem. And it was not too long a time until I saw all this from the air and on the ground. I came to one conclusion very soon. It is never easy for a bull moose to beget a calf.

Most animals mate in secret and nobody, except for a few naturalists, ever see the actual act. Most people merely see the result next spring when the miracle of life begins for the cute little offspring. But moose are different and everything appears to be comparatively out in the open. There are certain rituals between the competing bulls before the mating act can be accomplished. There are certain rules to follow. That, of course, was what I wanted to see

I had seen other horned or antlered animals fight for the privilege of mating with the females, but these other species seemed to go about it rather in a hurry and somewhat haphazardly.

In Colorado I watched mule deer bucks fight. The challenger suddenly ran out of the brush and quickly engaged the herd buck I was watching. The two fought furiously, their horns clacking. Their movements were almost too fast for the eye to follow. Then suddenly it was all over, with no apparent damages. The challenger quickly ran away and that was it.

In Alaska I once guided a couple men who wanted a movie of the caribou during rut. I got them right into the middle of a great herd, then stood guard while they got their pictures. Here the bulls seemed to mosey along fairly close to each other with no bother until two of them would suddenly start a fight. They fought furiously and very rapidly for perhaps half a minute, then quit; I could not tell which one was the winner for sure.

I wanted to see firsthand how moose went about it all. Old time Alaskans had told me how moose would start building a harem of cows; beginning, perhaps, around the 20th of September each year. This buildup would continue for around ten days; then the cows were ready and the actual rut would begin. Apparently, the cows went right along with this all right, becoming herded together at the insistence of one big bull. The cows went right on feeding together, paying no attention to the antics of the bull. The bull, however, guarded his harem with his very life. He neither slept nor ate much during this period. He lived off his body fat and thus became lank and poor as he jealously guarded his cows. Invariably, two bulls, each with a small harem, would meet and fight furiously. According to the rules it was "Winner take all." The defeated bull would lose all his cows to the winner and have to move elsewhere and start all over. With this method, a consistent winner of battles would soon gain a harem of magnificent proportions.

This was nature's way of taking care of a species. The bull that fathered the calves would be the biggest, healthiest specimen of all, and therefore the best father.

I did not doubt the authenticity of these old timers' tales, but decided to try and see it all myself.

The first opportunity came sometime in the 1950s when I glanced down from the air and saw two bulls fighting in a little clearing in the spruce timber. They were going at it furiously and very powerfully. With lowered heads they rushed together very rapidly with enough drive to sometimes force them both to their knees. Then they backed off and did it all over again.

Each bull tried to feint and get to the exposed side of the other, but a rapid parry would take care of that and the horns would crash again. Such magnificent power! Such drive! Two huge animals, weighing almost a ton each, going about it very seriously.

The fight ended with the loser suddenly moving off and, from the air, I could not properly see just why he was defeated, but he certainly must have been. I became determined to see all this from the ground someday.

A set of locked antlers from two unlucky combatants.

A perfect opportunity emerged in the early 1960s as I was flying down Chichokna Creek toward the main fork of the Chetaslina River in the Wrangell Mountains. On my left, in sparse brush and timber, I spotted a few cow moose feeding together. Then I saw a bull off on the edge with his head held high. I realized that I was observing a moose harem and a herd bull. Suddenly, I saw a flash in the distance and noticed it was another bull which had flashed his nearly white antlers in the sun. This other bull was apparently challenging the herd bull to do battle as he dipped his head, slashed at the brush, and pawed up great clods of tundra and earth. I had no doubt he was grunting as well—as bulls will do.

Moose do not bugle as an elk will when signifying readiness for battle, but they can grunt loudly and raise a great ruckus with their brush-slashing—making sounds which will carry a great distance in a silent forest.

Moose were plentiful in the 1960s. Understanding their habits improved hunting success.

The herd bull took up this challenge, I noticed. He pawed the ground, uprooted a few small trees, and created a turmoil. Then, as I circled, the two started toward each other—moving by sound since they could not see each other. There was no hurry about this. They merely got closer to each other, stopping every so often to slash at some brush.

In my circles it seemed to me they were both moving toward a distant clearing in the forest, not directly toward each other. Yet they were definitely getting closer and I decided to see as much of this as possible from the ground.

I flew over and quickly landed on the nearby Chetaslina River airstrip. This was the place we had built for the great Hal Waugh, Alaska's number one Master Guide, a year or so previous. There was no one there at the time so I just parked in the middle of the strip.

I needed to got across Chichokna Creek, which was rushing along, but was not quite prepared for a crossing. However, on board was a bag of clothing which contained some heavy wool socks. I took these and my rifle and rapidly walked to the creek. I removed my own boots and socks, donned the heavy wool ones, and safely crossed the creek without cutting my feet on the sharp stones. Then, with my own boots back on, I was ready to begin my rapid, though silent-as-possible, stalk.

Almost immediately I heard the two bulls as they grunted deeply and loudly. They pawed and slashed as they slowly moved together. This noise on their part helped give me the proper direction.

I did not know if the antagonists would hold the show until the audience arrived or not so I moved quickly, though silently. I did not even want them to know they had an audience for that matter. And I very nearly blew it all by getting too close to the herd bull. He veered around a particularly thick patch of spruce timber and I nearly ran right into him. Yet luckily, I saw him first and was able to successfully crawl away on my belly and get away from him. He probably was not interested in me anyway, but I did not want any distraction at all if I could prevent it. Away from him once more I could move toward the clearing.

When I carefully arrived at the clearing the challenger was already there; standing alertly, grunting, and staring across with red-rimmed eyes. He was certainly in a rage and looked absolutely formidable to me.

Then the herd bull arrived. It was clear there was no big hurry to begin this battle. The rituals and rules must be followed to the letter. The two great bulls stood poised, one on each side of the clearing. They postured, flexed their muscles, moved sideways, and both urinated. I don't know why they did that, they both stunk to high heaven already; but I supposed this part of the ritual was meant to scare the living daylights out of each other. It was almost as if each was saying, "Look fellow, if you don't get the hell out of here, I am truly going to fix your clock; there wont be anything left of you except moose-burger!" or something like that.

They moved into the clearing slightly, heads lowered. Then, when it was obvious that neither was going to quit, at some undetectable signal they rushed at each other. They came together, their antlers meeting with a terrific impact. Such terrible power! The tremendous blow put them both on their knees. But not for long. They were both back on their feet instantly. Each had a bloody nose from that first terrific impact.

Then they whirled and came together again, their antlers taking such great punishment I couldn't see why they did not break. Each bull was trying to get at the side of the other, to gore him and do him in. But each was quick enough to turn and meet the thrust of the other head-on again.

They fought all over that arena, pushing with their antlers together. One time they were so close to me I was extremely uncomfortable, and terrified. Yet they moved away again. I had my rifle at the ready, but most certainly did not want to have the need of shooting one, or both, of them. Soon their powerful thrusts became a little slower as they tired. Then the herd bull got in a blow! He feinted toward the side of the other. The challenger turned to parry the blow, yet the right antler of the herd bull caught him in the side with a powerful, raking thrust. The challenger went down, but came right back up to meet the next thrust head-on.

The fight went on but the challenger did not have much drive left. His left side was now covered with blood. Suddenly he reared on his hind legs, whirled, and ran off. Through, finished, whipped—fairly and squarely.

The herd bull, in his moment of glory, stood at the side of the clearing, head lowered, and pawed up some tundra and dust. I figured he was just getting his breath. But perhaps he was saying, "And don't come back, you SOB, because if you do, I will pulverize you."

That day I had observed, from ringside, one of the greatest shows I had ever seen and was extremely glad the opportunity had been presented to me.

By the early 1970s my outfit, Wilson Air Service at Gulkana Airfield, had grown from a one-pilot, one-plane operation to something like a three-pilot, five-airplane operation. During spring, summer, and fall we were all very busy with very numerous flights.

We took care of geologists in distant locations, flew out gas for helicopters, and handled mountain climbing and scientific expeditions. In the fall we took care of a lot of hunters, both resident and nonresident. Since there was no scheduled airline service, my pilots made many trips into Anchorage to meet the airlines and fly out business executives, needed parts for all kinds of machinery, or hunters.

I flew the Super Cub, spotting people out in the no-airport wilderness locations—just about anywhere they wanted to go. These little, short-range flights were very numerous and kept me busy. As the boss, I had to spend part of the time in the office—too much of it. Yet I managed to crowd in a lot of flying.

My curiosity about big game animals had never diminished and I always observed them as much as possible as the Cub—at 90 miles per hour—flew over them.

Gulkana is situated almost on the banks of the Copper River. This river is very swift and wide during the summer and autumn high-water season. It is not easily crossed except by a good boat; there is no bridge. Therefore, just on the other side it is pure wilderness. There were no residents on that side of the river toward the Wrangell Mountains. But it was wonderful hunting country right on our doorstep. With airplanes, we went to all the mountain slopes and numerous beautiful valleys where hunting camps were located. This country and beyond was my domain. I jokingly referred to it as "my back yard," but then said I would allow other people to use it as long as they treated it with respect and didn't leave any old tin cans lying around.

Not far toward the slopes of Mt. Drum there existed an isolated moose herd. We had observed them, counted them, and knew their approximate range as well as the ratio between bulls, cows, and calves. It was a healthy herd and was seldom, if ever, hunted.

Higher up on the slopes where the timber thinned out there were other herds of moose that were being hunted with the use of track vehicles or horses. But this particular herd was farther down, in heavier timber, and harder to hunt. Since the other herds were numerous, everybody seemed satisfied with their luck and the isolated herd was left alone.

Moose are not migratory and, though the different herds do mingle, they mostly remain in their own bailiwick.

I flew over this herd on many flights while carrying a guide or hunter to, or from, hunting camps. One September I was busy, as usual, flying these trips and enjoying the beautiful autumn colors seen below. Then I saw the herd. There was the greatest harem of cows I had ever seen—perhaps twenty in all.

And there was a bull—a great, magnificent specimen—who was their lord and master. I figured he must be really something to command a harem of such proportions. On each flight I looked them up. I wanted to see just what was going on.

Off to the side at least a half mile away there were some smaller bulls, probably four or five of them. I reasoned these smaller bulls had probably been whipped by the big bull and their cows appropriated. These small bulls did not get very close to the herd or the big bull would take positive, devastating action.

Flying hunters and moose meat to and from camp required many trips—providing ample opportunity to observe the great game herds.

On one flight with a nonresident hunter I noticed another great bull, obviously a challenger, moving up-slope toward the herd. I circled him once to see if he seemed a worthy specimen—and he was. The hunter appreciated me showing him the moose, but I was not really doing this for him. I was studying the situation because I believed I was going to see a battle and I wanted to figure it out in advance.

Leaving the hunter off at his camp, I flew back there and slowly circled the herd. Moose are not disturbed when an aircraft circles over and pay no attention, unless you buzz them at a low altitude. Sure enough, the two bulls were going into their ritual and preparing for battle. They pawed the ground, uprooted a few small spruce trees, slashed the brush, and began slowly moving toward each other.

Then I noticed that these bulls seemed to be moving toward a little clearing in the forest again—not directly toward each other. How could these bulls know the clearing was there and that it would be a dandy, brush- and tree-free area to have their battle?

My memory fled back to my high school days when I had been laboriously studying American History. I learned that in Revolutionary War days all generals seemed to maneuver their slow-moving armies so their battle could take place in a large clearing. It was almost as if the opposing generals had sat at a conference table with a map between them and then said, "Now let's have our battle in this nice meadow." (Of course they didn't do that, but it seemed the battle occurred so the musket and bayonet-equipped soldiers could easily get at each other in open country.) But how could moose do the same thing? Yet, for the third time, I was seeing two antagonists moving toward a certain clearing as if it were all preordained. It is one of the questions about moose that I will never have answered.

I was determined to watch this battle, though it was going to be from the air this time since there was no place to land. I arranged it by going back to Gulkana, picking up another hunter, then taking on some extra fuel. I took him directly to his camp, then flew back to the moose herd alone. I was going to break one of my own rules here. As any charter operator, I had certain rules for pilots. One rule was that they were to fly directly to their destination with no dillydallying or sight-seeing on the way. They, for the most part, followed this rule, as did I. But this time, unknown to all, I was going to break that rule since I was going to watch that battle. I had adequate fuel for two or three hours if need be.

The two great leviathans, if they can be called that, moved slowly to the edge of the arena. Then following all the ritual and the rules, they postured and showed each other what a perfect rage they had developed and how absolutely invincible they were. When all had been done properly they faced each other, and their battle began. I could not hear their great antlers clashing, but I could plainly see it all. They fought in a magnificent manner.

As they circled and slashed and parried I could not tell for some time which bull might win since they were both of tremendous size and their antler growth was about equal. Yet I could easily tell them apart as they fought since no two sets of antlers are ever the same, and an experienced guide can spot the difference instantly. I just knew this fight was going to last for some time.

As I circled I saw movement from the corner of my eye and looked the other way. There was one of the small bulls from off in the fringes moving toward the cows. I watched him; he was just a very young bull with barely palmated antlers. Yet he was old enough and big enough to do anything a bull is supposed to do. He moved with his head held high as if he was following a scent, and I reckon he was. He moved right past several cows until he got to a certain one. Then he circled her and smelled her and I knew what he was going to do. Why, the little stinker! The audacity of it all! To go in there and steal a cow while the old herd bull was fighting for his very life and his harem, and could not do anything about it—unable to come run the imposter away.

The young bull did not waste much time with his love-making. There was not much time to waste either. I laughed and slapped the panel, and called him some more names. But I was very glad I had observed one more thing in the world of moose.

I got my eyes back on the battle, then noticed the fury was diminishing somewhat as the antagonists tired. Then the old herd bull suddenly got in his best lick. He knocked the challenger down, possibly goring him. The challenger got right back up, parrying one more thrust, but he was finished. He whirled to run off and the old herd bull jabbed him right in the butt with those terrible points. Wow! I'll bet that hurt! The challenger got away then and the old herd bull stood there with his head lowered, grumbling.

I looked back toward the herd then and the little bull had finished his little tete-a-tete with the cow. I was certain I could see a grin or smirk on his face, but moose don't grin, do they? Perhaps it was my overworked imagination or maybe it was because of a subtle change of light as the sun went under a little cloud. At any rate, the little bull was getting the hell out of there while there was still time.

The old bull turned then and slowly walked back toward the herd. He walked with just the right amount of swagger as is appropriate for one who has just completed another conquest. He was possibly the fightingest bull on that whole mountain.

He walked among his cows to show off a bit and see how they were doing. As I put the plane back up to cruising speed and headed for home, I thought: All is peaceful and tranquil in that old bull's world. Yet he does not know, nor will he ever know, that he has just become a cuckold to a little bull less then half his size and age!

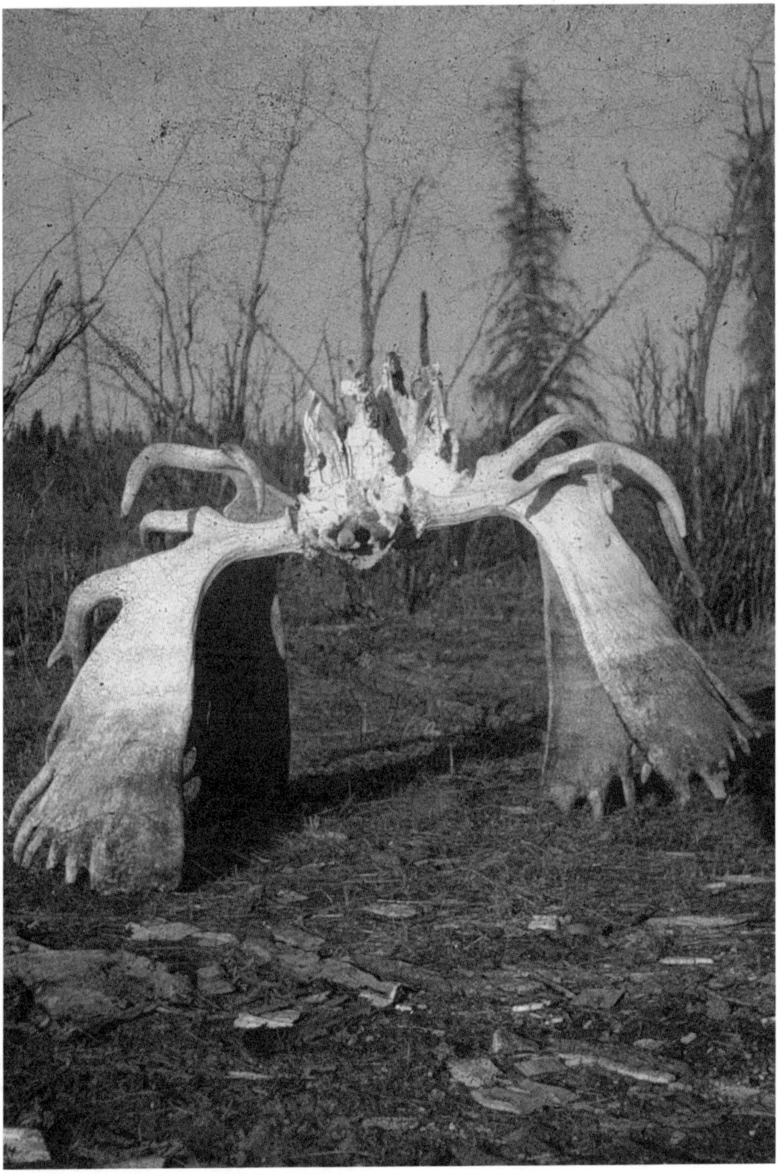

photo by Dave Widby

Experienced sheep hunters/guides, aware that bears also roam the tundra, always had to take precautions to protect sheep meat and capes.

CHAPTER 16
THE BEAR THAT WON

Most guides, outfitters, and bush pilots that spend a lot of time out in wilderness Alaska have bear stories to tell. If they are writers, sooner or later they write down a bear story—or several of them. The reason is obvious enough since there are a lot of bear in Alaska. Almost the entire south coast and a good bit of the west coast of the state are brown bear habitat. Many salmon streams enter saltwater along these coasts and the plentiful, spawning fish create extra food for bears. Bears also are vegetarians at times and feed on the lush plant life that grows on these damp coastlines. Black bear also inhabit coastal areas, yet do not mingle with the great brown bear.

In almost all of interior Alaska—except the very highest of the mountains—grizzly bears roam. The blackies are very numerous within the interior as well. Even beyond the land mass to the north and west, on the pack ice of the Arctic Ocean, the great white bear, or polar bear, roams—seldom coming ashore.

So if you happen to be a person who spends a lot of time in Alaska's great outdoors, you are going to encounter bears quite often, whether you want to or not. Under careful game management many bears are shot each year to become trophies for hunters. But the supply does not diminish at all so long as our biologists in the field are alert and control the hunting properly. As I said before, there are a lot of bears and they will remain numerous for many years to come. Bears are most certainly not endangered species within Alaska.

Having spent so much of my life in the wilderness for one reason or another I, too, have hunted bears as a guide for hunters. I often encountered bears while doing something else and did not want an encounter at all. Therefore, I could relate numerous bear tales, if motivated to do so. Bear stories can get boring, however, or so it seems to me; so I try to hold it down a bit and let the others jot down their stories.

In the interest of conformity, however, perhaps just one bear story could fill in a small part of this writing and not cause too much boredom. This bear story may not be as scary as some, only more vexing.

In 1967 I was doing the same as I had done for years—guiding two or three nonresident sheep hunters for trophies. During these periods I let my pilots at Gulkana take care of other flying matters, something they were well-qualified for. The sheep hunting, although very strenuous work, was sort of like a vacation for me; I loved to do it and looked forward to it eagerly each year. I also took many fly-in hunts, as many as could be crowded in each year. These fly-in hunts were for residents of the state who did not hire a guide. It was a matter of taking these men, or women, out to a place where trophy class Dall rams were known to exist on the mountains above where we landed. The hunters were on their own after being spotted out where their hunt could begin. I always asked them to please take nothing less than a full curl; if they were inexperienced, I always showed them pictures of large rams and explained how to tell a full curl from a younger, three-quarter, or seven-eighths curl ram. The success rate for these resident hunts was not too good, since many of the hunters did not know just how to go about it. Yet they tried, and learned. About the second or third time around they usually scored with a nice trophy.

For the nonresidents we booked up a fully guided hunt, of course, which cost much more. We went after the big trophies, always the full curl, and the best we could find. We never took anything less than that on a guided hunt, unless the hunter became confused and shot a small one by mistake. This did not happen often.

"It was a matter of taking these men, or women, out to a place where trophy class Dall rams were known to exist on the mountains above where we landed." Lorene Ellis with a ram in 1963.

In 1967 I had decided to take two rams from the Kotsina drainage, at that time a primitive area with no mining roads as yet built into the main valley. There were not really a lot of rams there, yet I knew of a few very good trophies and hunting pressure in the area was not very great. There was a good possibility of an undisturbed hunt or two.

The particular hunter I booked for one of these hunts was the usual nonresident: he was a city man and was all gung ho, at first, to get out there and start "roughing it," as they called it. To us, if we had a comfortable base camp to return to, it was not roughing it at all—just a normal way of life.

This hunt started out well enough. On the first hunt the hunter missed his shot, probably due to excitement or buck fever, and he did not have a chance for a second shot. The ram vanished. I decided, however, since this was early in the hunt and we had ample time left, to give him a second chance.

Carl Asplund was my packer, but did not accompany us on this second hunt. He was busy packing in a spike camp we had used previously. Carl was a good man, a very good packer, and a good companion in the wilderness. While he would not actually guide a hunter, he could have done so, but chose not to be a guide. He did all he could, actually more work around camp than I ever asked for.

The hunter and I crossed Roaring Creek without getting our feet wet and started up the mountain; myself with a small pack on my old packboard—consisting mostly of our lunch and raincoats. Hunters, while required to carry their own rifle, were not asked to carry anything else unless they volunteered to do so.

This time we got up into the hunting country above the brush line where I soon spotted the rams I was looking for from a great distance. It took us quite some time maneuvering around them to stay out of site and get slightly above them before beginning our stalk. It started to drizzle, not very hard, but wet nevertheless; so we put on our raincoats.

By this time the hunter was beginning to complain a lot about the entire idea of hunting and he wanted nothing more than to get it over with and get out of there. We had made him as comfortable as possible, yet he did not sleep well and seemed to dislike camp life after all. I told him to hang in there and we would get him a good sheep. After all, that was why we had come—the only purpose in fact. He said he would make sure this was his last day. All he seemed to want was to get back to a motel, put on clean clothing—after a shower, and go down to the cocktail lounge and restaurant. To him that was the only way to live, not climbing around on steep mountains in quest of pesky white rams. I had difficulty understanding this man and why he had come at all. Yet if he quit without getting a ram it would have been a useless effort, and the hunt would have cost him just as much anyway. I really hoped this hunt would be successful on this day, as it looked as if I could not hold him for a longer period.

We finally got in position, as I determined after crawling up to peek over a ridge in the wet tundra. I got the hunter up there, pointed out the best full curl ram, and made him take his time. This time his shot went true and we had it! I always had a feeling of elation when a hunter got his ram, especially with one shot. There is a definite feeling of satisfaction when this occurs. Of course it also meant that my work was to begin as soon as the hunter got the trophy. The next thing was to get the trophy itself back down the mountain in a form that would be presentable to a taxidermist for mounting.

I went about it, ignoring the rain entirely. That did not bother me at all. I carefully removed the cape from the shoulders forward and skinned the entire head very carefully. The hunter complained and wanted me to hurry, but I was not to be hurried during this work. A guide that is worth his salt will take all the time necessary to complete this task, as well as to remove the horns and upper part of the skull from the remainder of the skull.

This done to my satisfaction, I turned to the carcass and started skinning and gutting it. The hunter complained mightily about this, saying, "Leave that damn thing, I don't want the meat anyway."

I told him that he was paying for this part anyway and that we always kept the meat. Wanton waste was a violation of the law and we always brought in the meat. I did not elaborate on the fact that we valued sheep meat more than any other kind of wild meat. The meat off those big rams is the best meat of all and we would be sure to save all of it, if at all possible. So I went about it all and ended up by cutting the carcass in two pieces by separating the hindquarters from the front quarters. These I placed on a flat rock where they would stay clean. It was raining on them, yet rain will not hurt meat for a short while; we would make sure to have this meat down off the mountain the very next day, get it hung in a dry spot, and it would be fine.

I wanted to take some of the meat along. Yet with the hunter in such a tizzy to get off that mountain I decided that a heavier pack would slow us down some, so I left it all and merely loaded the cape and horns on my packboard. I removed my raincoat since I did not want to be sweating along with it on. I could stand to get a little bit wet in the drizzling rain.

We got down off the mountain, to the river, and before we reached base camp I could see Carl had preceded us. Anticipating our arrival in a very wet condition, he had brought in a lot of dry wood for a big fire and had erected an extra tarp for a shelter. When he saw us coming, he nudged the coffee pot a little closer to the heat and had hot coffee waiting for us. This was all very welcome and seemed the best in comfort to me. We could sit under the tarp on handy logs, sip coffee, and really live it up. I was happy to stay right there.

Yet we had not been there five minutes when the hunter asked me to get the airplane ready so we could depart right away. I couldn't talk him out of it any longer, so I got his trophy and gear in the airplane and we left. Before departing, I told Carl I would see him early the

THE BEAR THAT WON   169

next morning and that we would have a full day to go back up the mountain for that meat.

I managed to keep the hunter around long enough so I could flesh the cape and prepare it for shipment to his taxidermist—after salting and wrapping it properly; then he was on his way in a rental car. I was not especially unhappy to see this hunter depart.

Early the next morning I flew back to base camp and met Carl. We were really looking forward to getting all that sheep meat down where we could eat some of it, since we had been out of meat for a few days. The rain had quit and a beautiful day was starting. We did not even take our raincoats, just our packboards and rifles. Rifles always accompanied us due to the possibility of meeting up with a mad bear in the brush or something. The rifles were as much a part of us as they are to soldiers.

One of the "...or somethings." that made guides always carry their guns in sheep country. Wolverines are powerful, agressive meat thieves.

Getting above the brush line, we could hear Roaring Creek far below us with its well-named roar. Just a small stream during low water, it could be a torrent after a large cloudburst in the mountains. Even when small, it roared anyway, keeping up its namesake as it cascaded down through its steep canyon.

We eased on up the mountain and soon were getting close to the sheep carcass. Then, further up the mountain, I saw a bear—a grizzly. It was coming our way, pacing along as a bear will do, followed by two small cubs that were running as hard as they could to keep up. They seemed to be headed directly toward our sheep meat, as we were.

"Damn it all," I said, "That old bear is going toward our meat, sure as we're born. I am going to try and head that old gal off." I kneeled and carefully sighted ahead of her. I did not want to shoot the bear. Even had the bear season been open, which it was not, it would have been illegal, and stupid as well, to shoot a female bear with two small, helpless cubs. So I shot in front of her and she shied and jumped the other way, but then she lined out and just kept coming right on toward that meat.

"Come on." I said, "Let's see if we can beat her to that meat." Carl, a taciturn man not given to noisy outbursts of speech, said nothing, but merely quickened his pace.

But we were too late. The bear beat us to the meat and, although we had gotten close, she ignored us entirely. She ran up to those hindquarters, grabbed them in her teeth, then stood up while gulping away. She bit a great chunk out, then flung the quarters away from her, down off the rock into the dirt. The little cubs scrambled after it and started gnawing on it. The sow then grabbed the front quarters and repeated her previous performance. I was cussing up a noisy storm by then, but it did no good at all. A couple more bullets in her direction did nothing at all to faze her either. In desperation I ran around to the right. There was a steep little ravine there and I could get a little closer to her by keeping the ravine between us. I actually got within rock-throwing distance and managed to hit her with one, then she bristled up and charged. I was afraid Carl might have to shoot her, but he patiently stood there with his rifle trained on her while she started to cross that ravine; the cubs right behind her.

She knocked off the charge before getting up on my side of the steep little ravine, turned around, and went back to mauling and eating the sheep meat. We were defeated and we well knew it. I looked at Carl and he was silent as always, just watching the destruction.

Soon we knew the meat was ruined and with a few more cuss words on my part, we left the area; leaving it all for that damned old bear. I just hoped she would get a bellyache from eating too much fresh meat.

Do you like corned beef? Well I am not absolutely crazy about it, but that is what we had that night, along with some other fixings. It was all the meat we had. Up on the mountain a happy old bear and her cubs were glutting themselves on the choicest meat to be found anywhere.

She had won that round and fairly enough I suppose, when you come to think about it. Bear often go up on the sheep mountains for whatever reason they might have. If a bear can get a whole sheep carcass and bluff two men out of it, why, more power to her—I guess. Bears have to live, too. The male bears make great trophies to certain hunters that want one, but not nearly all the hunters even want to take a bear. They are out there when wanted and there would not be any great male trophies if we were allowed to shoot the sows with cubs. The regulation prohibiting this killing is a very sensible one.

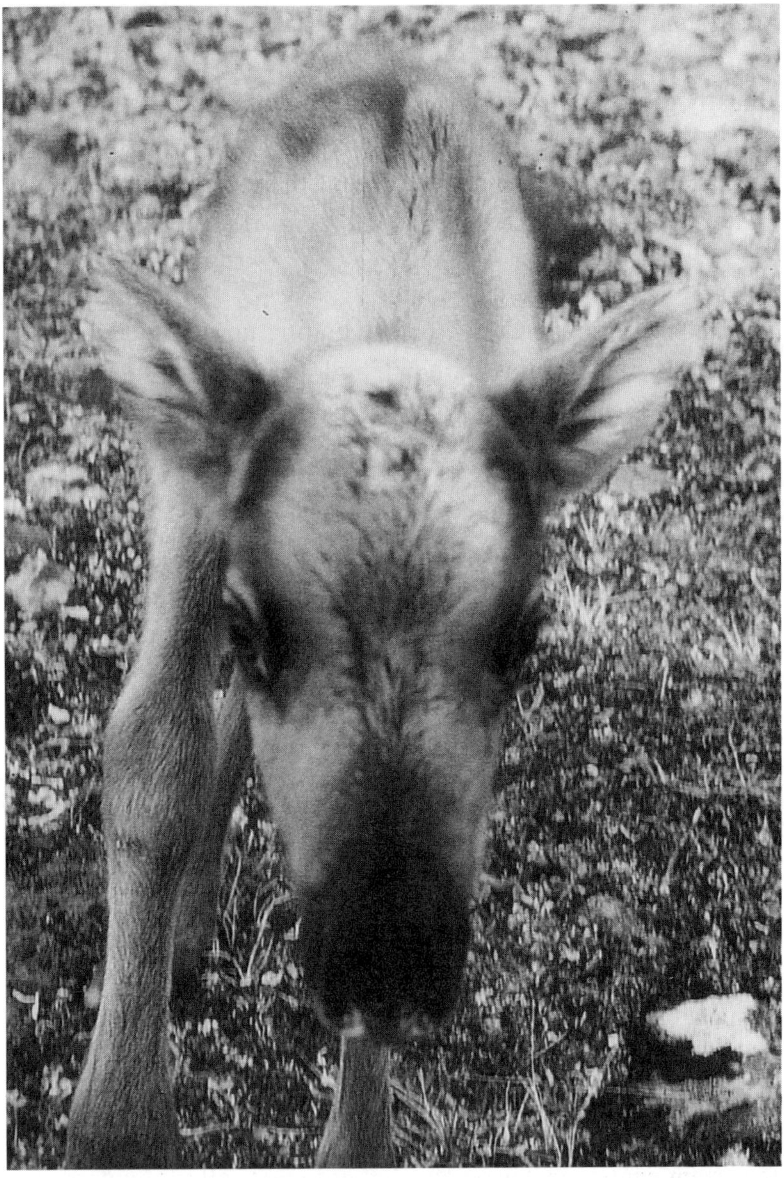

CHAPTER 17
CARIBOU ARE STRANGE BUT MARVELOUS CREATURES

At certain times of the year in Alaska you can sit out on the tundra on high ground and watch caribou migrating. You can start in the morning, just at sunrise, and sit there all day until after sunset and there will still be caribou going past your observation point. Ceaseless, unending, caribou in motion always. They will not be bunched up as some animals might be, such as elk moving from their summer mountains toward their winter range, but there will always be caribou in sight. They will be traveling scattered out in small bunches and there will always be more coming. They do not hurry, fut feed as they go. It is a wondrous sight, something never seen in other parts of the world, except perhaps in a very few places where there are many thousands of animals.

In fact, caribou migrate constantly. Their big migrations are in the spring and again in the fall between their summer and winter ranges, but in between these times they are always going somewhere. The migration may be very slow and seemingly aimless, but they will always be moving. Like the buffalo of long ago, they are always on the move and do not overgraze their range. They feed as they go, but never stop and stay in one place.

In winter, most of the herds move into the big timbered areas of

Alaska. There they remain until spring, when the cows move out toward the calving grounds. During these winter months they move around slowly, yet constantly. You never know just where they are going since their movements are unpredictable, but they will be on the move always. It has been determined they move in a clockwise direction, but due to the way they wander here and there it takes a long time to see that the direction is actually clockwise.

In winter, a pilot with experience at tracking can easily locate a large herd by flying the perimeter of the tracks. It is not necessary to actually see many of the animals themselves, just the perimeter of their range as seen by the tracks. For a large herd this may take several hours in a fairly fast airplane.

There are many different caribou herds in Alaska, some of them tremendous in size. The Western Arctic herd is the largest one, numbering an estimated 450,000 animals, followed by the Mulchatna herd at an estimated 250,000. There are many other large herds such as the Porcupine, Nelchina, Forty-Mile, and so on. There are also many small herds, some of them with only about 2,500 animals. Caribou range over a great part of our great state clear to the coastal areas, including the Arctic. All combined, the estimate is over a million caribou within the state, and that is a great amount of animals.

Our own herd, the Nelchina in the great Copper River Basin and extending west to McKinley Park, varies in population from year to year from perhaps only 30,000 animals on up to about 70,000. State game management tries to maintain the herd at about 50,000 animals so the herd number will not become too large for the range available. They generally keep it within reasonable limits by regulating hunting seasons.

In Alaska we have barren ground caribou. Northern Canada has other subspecies, however; in that vast country caribou roam through it all the way to the east coast. There are the woodland, the mountain, and the Quebec-Labrador caribou in Canada. There are also many barren ground caribou in Canada as well. The great herds roam freely across the border between Alaska and Canada, back and forth during their endless migrations. In my area of Alaska our caribou of the Nelchina herd sometimes take off and go to Canada during the winter months; often to the consternation of residents that would like to hunt them to help fill up the freezer with fresh meat.

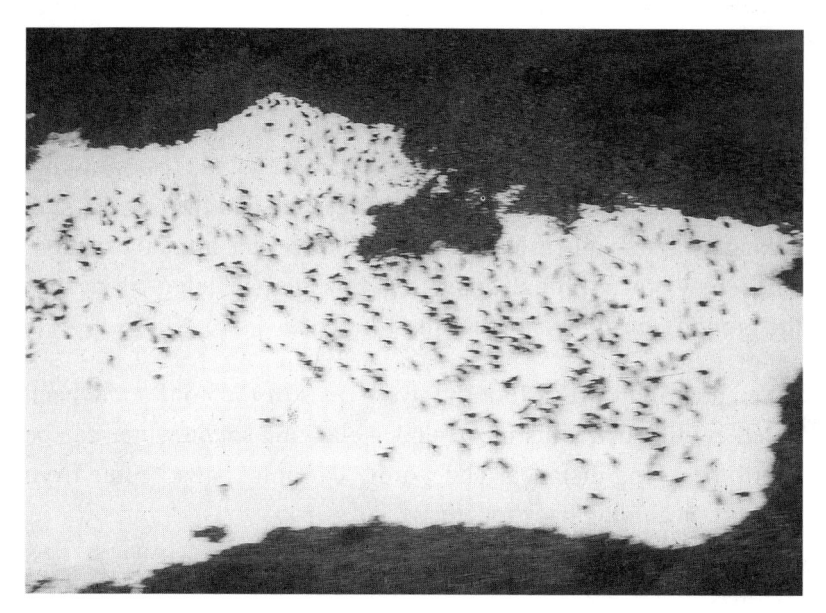

This herd of caribou is trying to get away from the flies and the heat of summer by standing on a mountaintop snowfield at 6,000 ft. elevation.

For centuries Alaska Natives have hunted caribou for subsistence. There is evidence of them killing caribou many centuries ago when their only weapons were very primitive, such as double-ended spears. It is said they made barriers to trap the caribou, then used these spears to kill them. The modern day Eskimos and Indians use modern firearms, of course, and take the caribou at will. Natives have traditionally used all of the caribou—utilizing every part possible, not just the lean meat. They even utilize the small intestines and the contents of the belly. The white man is more inclined to keep only the lean meat and therefore does not get the food value needed to survive with caribou as the main diet. The Natives, however, using all the animal get a much more complete diet from the animal and survive very well.

Caribou are much different than other deer-like animals. A caribou will not stand very high, yet they are stocky creatures and possibly weigh as much or more than a mule deer. They do not have dainty little hoofs such as other deer. Their hoofs are nearly as big as a cow. When the caribou puts weight on a foot the split hooves spread out, enlarging the area which the foot makes contact with the ground. This helps greatly to keep the animal from sinking down into the soft tundra or other soft ground and they do not sink through snow so much. With those big hooves the animal can more easily paw down through snow to get lichens (which grow next to the ground) during winter months.

When a caribou lifts a foot the two halves of the hoof come back together with a very distinct sound, a clacking sound which can be heard for a long distance. The words "caribou clatter" come from the hooves coming back together.

Both male and female caribou have antlers. On bulls the antlers are tremendous, with many points on each antler, a great spread, and at least one "shovel" on the brow. These shovels are vertical rather than horizontal—such as the brow palms on moose. Caribou usually have only one shovel, in place of another one on the other antler there will just be a brow tine. It is estimated only one bull in five thousand with have a double shovel.

The antlers on a cow are quite small, similar to the antlers on a small deer. The cows carry their antlers all winter and do not shed them until spring, at the beginning of the calving season. The bulls, however, shed their antlers in the fall after the rutting season is over. The antler shedding period starts in late October and continues past November tenth for most of them. A few bulls carry their antlers until late winter.

"Caribou are curious animals and can actually be tolled up at times in the same way antelope are hunted."

A nonresident hunter is not required to be accompanied by a guide to hunt either moose or caribou in Alaska. However, it is wise to have a guide along or at least a friend who is an experienced hunter and knows how to quickly judge the value of the antlers. A hunter who is used to hunting deer or elk in the Lower 48 will be amazed at the antler size of caribou and is likely to shoot a quite small bull, thinking his antlers are actually very big.

The same thing applies to moose. An experienced guide or hunter can quickly evaluate the antlers' value and tell a novice hunter if it is a worthy animal to be taken. Too many hunters have taken small-antlered caribou or moose by not having someone along to help look at the antlers and advise if it is a worthy animal or not.

Caribou are curious animals and can actually be tolled up at times in the same way antelope are hunted. While I never took a caribou that way, we did—at times—have fun sitting on a high knoll up in the tundra and bringing a caribou or two within rifle range. All we did was place a jacket over a rifle barrel while sitting there and waving the rifle back and forth occasionally. It sometimes works very well. They are interesting animals to hunt and it sometimes is not too difficult to get a good caribou, if you happen to be in the right place at the right time as they move endlessly across the country.

It turned out that I was the pilot chosen to do the flying when the Department of Fish and Game wanted to find out just when the caribou started shedding their antlers in the fall of each year. They decided on a method which would take quite a bit of flying time, but which would be effective.

In mid-October our large Nelchina herd was on their annual fall migration to their winter range. We caught the herd as they were moving above timberline south of the Denali Highway past Dickey Lake; then on toward Paxson Lake where they would swing to their right and spread out in the timbered area of the great Copper River Basin.

The biologist instructed me that we were to fly out, locate the herd, then circle over them until he had counted 200 bulls. When that had been accomplished we would quit for the day. At first I did not quite understand just why we were doing this, but soon caught on. He wanted to see which day we would find one or more of the bulls with shed antlers.

Bulls can easily be distinguished from cows since their antlers are tremendous—much larger than the antlers on the cows. Also, the bulls have an off-white neck, easily noticed from the air. Their heads remain black, but the white neck easily distinguishes them from the cows.

After a few days of this business of counting 200 bulls each day, one day we saw a bull with only one antler and it happened to be on October 22. That fact was marked on his clipboard and we continued on the next day. On that day we saw at least three bulls with only one antler each; then after that we began to see bulls with both antlers shed. The biologist had found out what he wanted— that the bulls definitely started shedding antlers in late October.

". . . the bulls definitely started shedding antlers in late October."

For a period of time after Alaska gained Statehood in 1959 we could still hunt the same day we were airborne. As stated, this was not truly sportsmanlike at all. Yet it was a very good way of getting your winter meat, especially where caribou were concerned. At that time, with our Nelchina herd we were allowed to take three caribou each year on our license. The season was lengthy: starting in August, going right through the winter, and ending on March 31. I had killed two animals during one season and when the month of March arrived could still take one more animal. It would be nice to have some fresh meat—the cows actually start putting on a small amount of fat in March and are quite good eating. So I decided I had better get a caribou before the season ended.

I was returning to my base at Gulkana one afternoon after having flown a charter up to the north somewhere. I was alone in the airplane and had my scope-mounted .30-06 rifle with me so I decided to swing out over the frozen lakes west of the airport and find some caribou. They were numerous in the timber and lake area and would be easy to get.

In winter the caribou liked to get out on a big open lake when they wanted to lay down and rest. Caribou may not be very smart critters, but they have the sense to bed down out on an open lake when resting. That way, they can see when wolves are coming and get away from them. They like to bed down out on a lake in the warm, late-winter sunshine and have a good rest.

So I eased around with the airplane and found what I was looking for, about 30 head of caribou bedded down on a large, frozen lake. I circled them once, which does not disturb them, then landed and stopped about 200 yards from them. They stood up but did not run. I took my rifle out of the airplane and kneeled down to study them. Some of them were bunched up rather closely and I did not want to shoot right into the herd, since there is a possibility of a bullet passing right through one animal and either wounding or killing another one. So I chose a cow that was standing alone with no other animal behind her and shot her. One clean shot was all it took and she was down.

When I shot the cow the herd all took off with a great clatter of their hoofs and were soon gone. I climbed in the airplane, started it up, and taxied over there to the fallen cow and stopped. It was then that I noticed another small caribou lying there about 50 feet away and I wondered what was wrong. I knew I had not shot it by accident, but there it lay. So I took my rifle and walked over to it. There I could see that it was still alive since it was breathing. I had thought that it was probably sick or something and perhaps I had better shoot it to put it out of its misery.

A happy caribou hunter.

Before shooting, however, I walked over and poked it in the belly with my rifle. That little caribou opened its large brown eyes and looked at me. Then those same eyes seemed to register pure panic! It suddenly bounded to its feet and I have never seen an animal run as fast as that one did to get away; it was gone instantly!

I stood there, then, and figured it all out. Why, that little caribou had merely been sound asleep, nothing wrong with it at all. Animals usually sleep with one eye open—so the saying goes—to watch for danger and wake up at the slightest sound. Yet this animal had slept through the noise of me landing the airplane not very far away; it had snoozed on when I shot the cow within a few feet of it; then had slept soundly when the herd took off with their hooves making a great, noisy clatter; and it had still slept when I taxied the noisy airplane up to within 50 feet of it. All that racket and it had still slept! Why, if I had been a wolf, I would be having dinner by now.

Caribou are strange creatures for sure.

In 1963 the Department of Fish and Game wanted a biologist to go out to the calving grounds and observe the caribou during the birth of the calves on our Nelchina herd.

The calving grounds at that time were in the Talkeetna Mountains in the vicinity of the Fog Lakes and south of the Susitna River. As the pilot it would be my job to find a suitable place to land out there with a Super Cub; sometimes a rather tricky thing. However, we were lucky in that respect. The winter snow was all gone in the area, but there was still ice remaining in an ideal spot. A small creek had "glaciered up" during the winter months. Water had run out over the ice but under the snow, spreading out further and further in the shallow little valley until the whole flat was covered with ice. A lot of this ice still remained and with my hydraulic wheel/skis it was an ideal spot to land safely.

With that accomplished we proceeded up onto high ground nearby to observe the caribou. The biologist—Jack Didrichson—was equipped with a clipboard, a spotting scope with tripod, and several tally counters in his pocket. I don't know just what all he wanted in the way of data, but part of it was to count cows with antlers and cows without antlers since the cows shed their antlers during the calving season. He would also count cows with calves and other needed data. As he proceeded with his work I merely stood by and watched. It was marvelous. There were caribou in all directions—constant movement. Using field glasses I could easily see cows that were lying down in the process of birth; cows standing with newborn calves lying at their feet as they licked the calf and waited for it to get up; and cows moving on with tiny calves wobbling along on shaky legs.

It was a great show and I was lucky to be able to participate in this.

We moved around to get other views, but always there were caribou—hundreds of them—in all directions. We would come upon tiny calves lying down and Jack had warned me about them. The little things, upon seeing us, would think we were the mother and try to come to us. I was told to avoid them and not let one of them touch me since the mother might reject the calf if the human scent got on the calf.

We came upon a tiny calf lying under a small bush and I decided to get a picture of it. I squatted down to do this and suddenly the calf got to his feet—surprisingly fast—and started toward me. I actually fell over to avoid it, but managed to snap the picture anyway. Then I managed to scramble away from it.

We spent several hours there while Jack did his work, then he was finally satisfied and we were on our way. We circled the great herd, observing it, and I realized it would be next to impossible to accurately count these animals in the conventional manner. There were just too many of them, caribou all over the place—most of them moving. Actually they use aerial photos to count the large herds in Alaska. About every other year an airplane takes vertical photos of the herd and the animals are counted on the ensuing photos. The fringes of the herd are counted with either fixed-wing aircraft or helicopters; the bulls are identified and counted as well.

This method of counting makes a reasonable estimate of the amount of animals in a herd, yet it is still just an estimate. It works very well, however. Since the count is always done in the same manner it reveals the trend to show whether the herd is increasing or decreasing. This gives the Fish and Game Department very necessary data to help with good game management.

We kept circling to observe the herd and suddenly we came upon a drama. It was late May and the weather was getting hot. The snow was rapidly melting in the mountains and there were numerous streams of meltwater running off in otherwise dry streambeds. Some were mere trickles while others were raging, swift torrents. We noticed a cow approaching one of these torrents and watched.

Caribou are good swimmers and have no fear of water. During migrations caribou will sometimes swim right across a lake rather than go around it. So this cow did not hesitate when she came to the stream, but stepped right in. The cow swam right across the swift stream, then stopped and waited for her calf to follow. And the little fellow did not hesitate, but stepped right in. The current immediately took it downstream and we were horrified. We were certain it would drown and wondered how an animal could be so stupid as to expect a tiny calf to swim such a torrent. However, as we circled we could see the little thing bobbing along as it went downstream, trying to swim across, but making very slow progress. It was swept past piles of driftwood and willows that grew along the stream and we were certain it would be drowned any minute. However, it was suddenly swept ashore and gained its footing, then managed to scramble out on the same side its mother was on. We were amazed and very pleased to see this.

That old cow did not come after the calf. It just stood where it was waiting for the calf to get across. The calf found its way upstream and found the mother, she smelled of it to make sure it was hers, then allowed it to get to her udder for some life-sustaining milk.

Then the cow and the calf went on their way as caribou always do; going somewhere, undoubtedly a happy pair and—as we thought—very lucky as well. It was a good day with a happy ending.

"On bulls the antlers are tremendous, with many points on each antler, a great spread, and at least one 'shovel' on the brow."

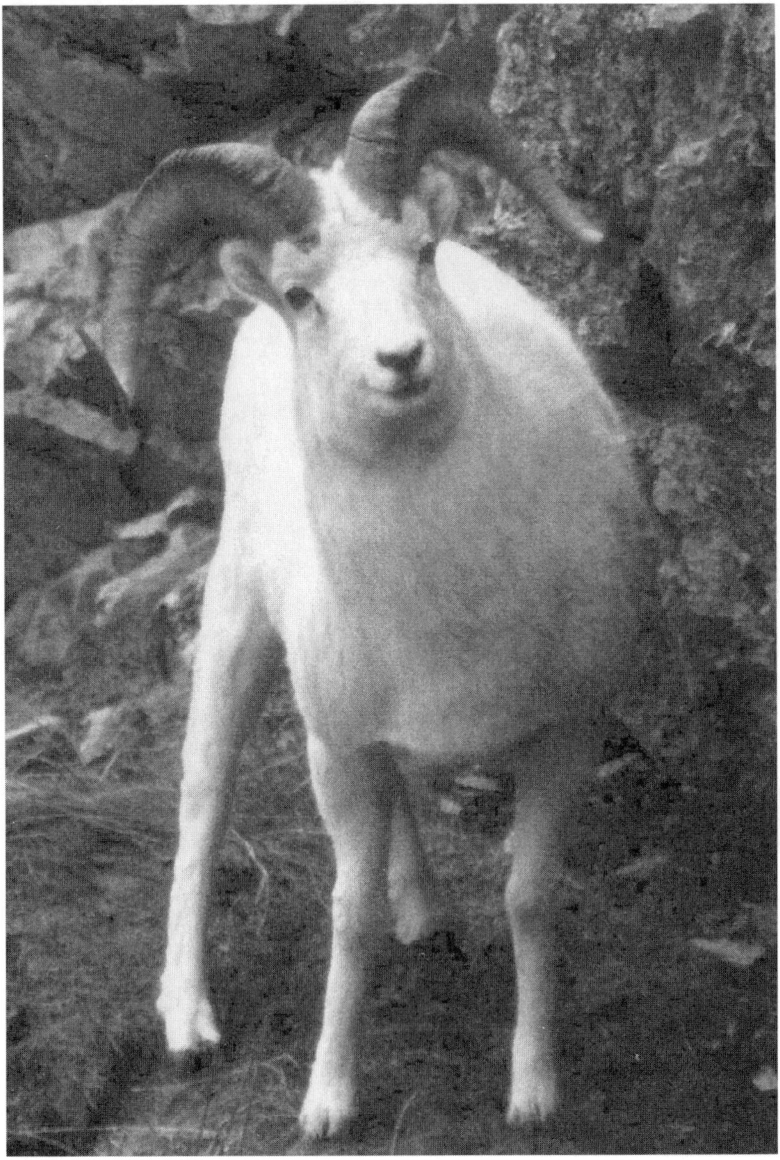

CHAPTER 18
FACTS ABOUT SHEEP AND HUNTING

Migratory Habits

Sheep are not generally considered migratory animals. It is true they have both a summer and a winter range, all of it being on one mountain system, and they do not move more than a few miles during the course of the year between these ranges.

Rams do move out at times, however, toward other ranges. During the summer months when the rams flock together away from the ewes, they often expand their range by moving out beyond what might normally be considered their range boundary. Older rams lead the younger ones on these excursions and they thereby expand their range into new territory.

I have seen rams in the spruce valleys, miles from any mountain system and they will be moving toward distant mountains. In such movements they mingle with other herds and become a part of them. Perhaps this helps prevent inbreeding. Ewes and the lambs will sometimes follow, but apparently not as much as the rams.

In summer the sheep roam on the high parts of their summer range and cover a large area. There may be overgrazing at times, but it is not a usual thing. When fall approaches they start moving down toward the winter range on a gradual basis. They get down quite low on the mountain, often down into the spruce timber. Here they winter.

The spruce offers protection from the cold winter winds and the sheep paw down through the snow for food, and sometimes during a tough winter live off their body fat. At times the winter winds remove a lot of the snow from the lower slopes and the sheep can move up and take advantage of this. They seek shelter under rimrocks when not feeding. Generally they winter quite well and, though they lose body weight, they are still able to get through until spring brings back the green feed. The lambs have the toughest time of it and many of them winterkill, but some always survive and make it through the winter.

As stated before, the new lambs are born down on this low winter range after the feed has started getting green. The new lambs make fast progress, especially if the mothers have wintered well. Lambs can soon follow as the sheep start their gradual movement up toward the summer range as the green feed appears ever higher on the mountain.

Market Hunting

In the early part of this century many mines were opened up in interior Alaska and many miners were hired to operate these mines. These men needed good food, thus, market hunters began furnishing meat for them. In the McKinley Park area there were reports of market hunting for sheep. This was probably done during a part of the year when the caribou—in their ceaseless migration—were too far away for meat harvesting; so sheep were substituted. But in the McCarthy/Kennicott area in the Wrangell Mountains there was no evidence to verify that market hunting had ever been done to help feed the very numerous men who mined for copper in the mountains or the men that operated the Kennicott copper mill. Yet fairly soon after I got started flying in the Wrangell Mt. area I found definite evidence of market hunting there. Perhaps stories exist about this market hunting, yet I never had come across it.

Piles of horns left over from market hunters consisted of single horns, probably brought down one at a time.

In 1957 I had become acquainted with the upper Chitina River from having flown sheep hunters to the area. I noticed an old cabin near the steep mountain just below the terminus of the extensive Chitina Glacier. This old cabin was on the old Martin Harrais mining claims and was still in pretty good shape. It had a metal roof and was dry and solid. I found out that a lady, Margaret Harrais, still lived—the widow of Marten Harrais. She was the Magistrate at the little town of Valdez down on the coast. I contacted her and worked out permission for the use of the cabin.

photo courtesy of Georgia Strunk

We chinked up the walls of the old cabin and cleaned it up. Then we furnished it with a Yukon stove, a Coleman lantern, and an aluminum cooking kit; it became a good place to use for a base camp. I was to use that cabin many times as the years wore on. It was also used extensively by others, with or without my permission.

In the yard near the cabin I noticed a great pile of sheep horns. These were individual horns that had been detached from the skull and brought in singly. They were very old and were peeling and discolored—some quite rotten. Yet they were fascinating and they told me a story. This pile of horns must have been left there by market hunters, taken many years before my time. Trophy hunters would have kept these horns, but there they were in that great pile. The market hunters must have packed them down off the mountain from carcasses of sheep that had been killed previously. The horn of the sheep is solid on the head when the sheep lives, yet after it has been dead for some time the horn loosens and can be removed by giving it a twist. I assumed that market hunters had carried these horns down off the mountain when they were up there hunting and had room to bring a horn down occasionally.

This all meant a lot of sheep were killed in this area, yet sheep were still very numerous in the area and some of the biggest rams ever taken would come from this country. Since that market hunting, the sheep—left alone except for the occasional trophy hunter—had multiplied and the herd strength was probably back to where it had been before the market hunting had taken place.

These were all great horns, most of them a full curl, and they showed me that—without a doubt—some of the largest Dall sheep in North America lived on these mountains.

I inquired around at McCarthy and Chitina, asking the old timers about market hunting and mentioned the great pile of horns near the old cabin below the Chitina Glacier. None of these old men could recall anything about market hunting except for one person. This was Bill Berry—now an old man—who had come to McCarthy when young and had set himself up in business as a mechanic and handyman. He had become a bootlegger during the prohibition days. He could recall pack trains going up toward Kennicott which might have been carrying sheep meat. And he knew for sure that packers had brought meat to the local brothel in McCarthy more than once. This is the only person who could fairly well verify that there were sheep meat hunters for the miners in the area. I always wished I could have found out more about this enterprise.

Broomed Horns

Few rams get through life without some horn damage. The tips of the horns are quite small and exposed to rough usage. When rams are battering heads together, as they do quite often throughout the year, they get a little off center on impact and the tip of a horn will break off. Also, they can break a horn during a fall in treacherous country. When the horn breaks, it shatters, and the remains of horn material are left sticking out and somewhat resemble the end of a coarse broom. Thus, the word "broomed." In time the rough ends of the horn wear off, leaving a smooth end larger than the original.

Bighorn rams have a problem with vision due to the horn growth obscuring their side or peripheral vision so they cannot see well to the side. When this happens they often rub their horn on a rimrock until it wears off, allowing vision to return. Also, bighorns will sometimes find that when their horns reach full curl the horns will reach the ground before their mouth and they cannot get to the feed which is very near the ground. Here again, they will rub their horns off so they can reach the good feed. Almost all bighorns are broomed, yet the thinhorn sheep, the Dall and the Stone, do not have as much problem and are not broomed nearly as much.

The horns on the World Record Dall ram taken by Harry Swank in 1961 were both broomed. Yet they were broomed evenly and it is hardly noticeable on the mounted head. When broomed unevenly, horns will not measure as high for the records.

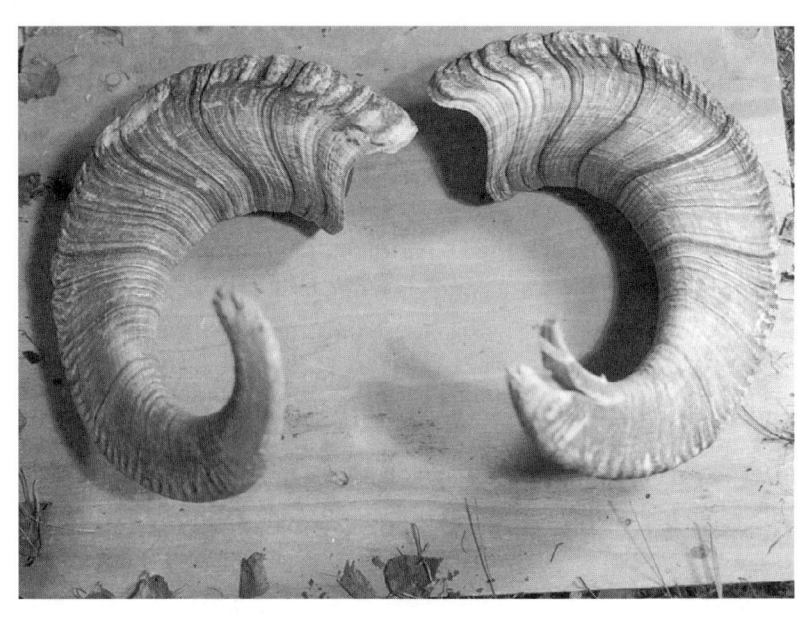

Broomed horns: the left one has been rubbed smooth; the one on the right has just recently been shattered and is still very rough.

Harvest Reports

When a hunter buys a big game license in Alaska he or she is allowed to take one male sheep of full curl horns or better on that license. Yet before going hunting for sheep, a harvest ticket is required as well. These harvest tickets can be acquired at the same place the license was bought and there is no extra charge for it. These are for statistical purposes and must be carried by the hunter and filled out properly when, and if, a ram is taken. It is a simple form to fill out and no hassle at all. When a ram is taken, a part of the harvest report must be attached to a major portion of the ram. It is to remain so until the horns and other parts of the sheep have been transported to the hunter's home.

These harvest reports are the best way for the Alaska Department of Fish and Game to determine how many rams are taken each year and are very important. After the ram is taken the harvest report must be filled out with the information of which drainage or mountain system the ram was taken in, along with other information.

This filled-out report can be mailed from anywhere and has the postage paid to make it easy. A reasonable time is allowed before it must be mailed back to the Department, but it must be done. From this information the state can determine how many rams are killed each year along with the area where the ram was taken. This count is quite accurate. It is very helpful for keeping records and seeing from year to year just how many sheep are taken.

Records show that in the 1970s there was an average of 1153 rams taken each year in Alaska, but the latest average for 1996 shows there were only 1074 rams reported taken in that year. That means less rams are being taken on an average basis now than there were several years ago. It enlightens us to the fact that hunting pressure is definitely not too heavy on the sheep. There should be good hunting for years to come and there will be full curl rams out there waiting to be taken by the hunter inclined to have a trophy ram.

Probably one of the reasons there are a few less sheep taken each year is because the record book hunters have quit searching for the extremely big rams they once pursued. After World War II ended and hunters could climb the mountains in Alaska at will in search of big sheep there were many hunters that felt they just had to get one of the largest rams ever taken—one that would point up big in the Boone and Crockett records. There was always the possibility that way out there somewhere would be a big old ram that beat them all and it would become a new world record. Many trophy hunters were like that and wanted nothing less that a real record book ram. Yet the new World Record ram taken by Harry Swank in 1961 has never been beaten, even after all these years. I believe many of the old hard-bitten trophy hunters have given up and no longer are after such big sheep nowadays. The days of the extremely big trophy are about gone. There are thousands of full curl rams left in some of the state, but none of them will go as high in the book as they did in older days. They are still very fine trophies and are coveted by many. There should be good hunting for these valuable and beautiful trophies for many years to come.

This group of all-record book rams is part of the display at the annual meeting of the Alaska Chapter of FNAWS in Anchorage, Alaska. All of the rams are over 170 pts. and most were taken in the '50s or '60's.

Harvest reports have helped game management to keep records on whether certain herds are increasing in numbers or declining. Certain herds do decline at times and studies are made to try and determine why this is so. At times it is difficult to see just what the reason is for the numbers going down in a certain herd. Probably the biggest reason is a tough winter, or perhaps several tough winters in a row, which reduces the number of sheep in the herds; but it is not always clear, at times, just what has made a herd go down in numbers. On the whole, however, the sheep population is quite well up in numbers and with good game management going on each year it will probably remain up in numbers.

Some of the big herds at the present time have few full curl rams left. These are generally the herds that are easiest to get to for the purpose of hunting. But remember, Alaska is tremendous and there are sheep on all the mountain ranges. Therefore there is a lot of country out there that still has full curl rams, it is just a little harder nowadays to find the right spot. Perseverance will do it, however. Research and correspondence with certain guides will give the potential hunter the information needed to get out there and locate a fine, full curl, trophy animal.

Rifles and Ammunition

There has been, and always will be, a lot of talk around the campfire about the "best" rifle for hunting sheep. But the fact is, there is no best rifle for this purpose. There are many, many rifles and most of them are good for the purpose of getting a trophy ram. Sheep are not large animals and are easy to kill.

It stands to reason that a good, flat-shooting rifle with a good scope will be better for the purpose than any other rifle. A rifle of .270 caliber with a 4X scope would be an ideal sheep rifle, for instance. Even the smaller, lighter .243 would be flat-shooting and ideal. But what I advocate here is that it is not necessary to go out and spend the money for a new rifle just for the purpose of getting a sheep. Any high-powered rifle will do.

photo courtesy of Georgia Strunk

This old timer has taken a huge ram with a lever action rifle with open sights—proving that any rifle will do.

When going through the process of booking up a hunter for sheep I always told the hunter to bring a rifle he was familiar with and that he liked to shoot. That, I believe, is the answer to the whole thing. A new rifle the hunter is not used to could turn out to be a detriment. Yet if the hunter just brings his old deer rifle that he has carried many times before that he is familiar with and likes—that is the rifle to bring.

I never learned much about ballistics, so when the campfire talk gets around to that subject I am merely a good listener. Yet having practiced a great deal with several different rifles, I know that I can hit what I am shooting at and am fairly adept at judging range, wind, and other factors. I am good enough to put a killing shot where it belongs and that is what counts in the long run. Though I was lucky enough that it was not necessary to pick up more than a couple of wounded rams during my career as a guide; it worked out all right and the job was done.

It is always necessary to have a good sling mounted on a rifle for carrying purposes. In the extremely rugged terrain where we hunt sheep, it is often necessary to have the use of both hands at once for reasons of safety and to help get on up to wherever it is you are going.

It all boils down to the fact than many rifles are good for the purpose of hunting sheep. While I would like to see a hunter come equipped with a flat-shooting, scope-mounted rifle; if he shows up with a .30-30 Winchester with open sights, that is all right with me. I could always get a sheep hunter within range so he could make a clean shot, even if his rifle was rather short of long-range capability. I never like the extremely long-range shots anyway. I do not care for shooting at sheep at a range of more than 200 yards, unless there is just absolutely no other way to get the job done. Generally it is not necessary.

As for ammunition, there is no doubt that if a hunter wants to handload his ammunition very carefully and accurately, that is fine. Yet factory loads are accurate and are very reliable. I would have liked to "rolled my own" ammunition, but since I never had time to settle down and do it properly, I depended on factory loads and never once had a failure.

For hunting and guiding sheep hunters I always carried my Husqvarna .30-06. This was a fairly light, very well-balanced rifle and I liked it fine. It did very well for me over a period of many years for sheep and other big game as well. One reason I always packed this rifle was for bear protection. Generally one does not need to worry about bear problems when hunting sheep on a high mountain. But it can happen, as you can see in the chapter I wrote entitled, " THE BEAR THAT WON."

Many sheep were taken by hunters before the development of magnum cartridges and variable-power rifle scopes.

At any rate, if a hunter showed up with a fairly small-caliber rifle that would not do the job on a bear, I always had the .30-06 to take care of any bear problem. I never worried about bear as long as I had that rifle in my hands. As long as you can shoot accurately—

and I could do that—the '.06 will take care of any bear that lives.

Harry Swank, who took the World Record Dall ram, always packed a .300 Winchester magnum. He most certainly did not need that caliber merely for sheep, but that is what he had. He had carried that rifle for every big game animal in Alaska; he was very familiar with it and an accurate shot. Therefore, that was the rifle he used and carried when he shot that big one in 1961.

So plan on bringing a rifle that you are familiar with and can shoot accurately. That is what is going to count and get the job done.

Physical Fitness

It seems quite obvious that if a person gets the idea of going sheep hunting, he or she would spend many hours over a period of a long time getting in good physical condition for the upcoming hunt. Consider that it may be necessary to climb a mountain so steep that it takes both hands, as well as the feet, to get where it is necessary to go for a successful hunt. Also consider that this sort of climbing might go on for hours—so good physical conditioning before the hunt begins is an absolute must. Yet some hunters do come who have not taken the time nor energy to get in really great condition.

Even in the heart of a big city it is easily possible to get the kind of conditioning necessary. A person can always jog each day—which certainly helps. Also there are always gymnasiums which have all sorts of equipment and machines that are helpful for achieving the fitness needed for a hunt.

During my long years as a sheep guide and outfitter I came to know that most nonresident hunters that would come hunting would either be middle-aged or getting close to it. That is obviously because the younger man—who might be in superb condition—does not usually have the funds to afford a sheep hunt. Most people have to work at a good job or profession for quite some years before he can have sufficient funds, along with the necessary time, needed for a hunt.

Trophies like these represent a lot of strenuous physical exercise during—and before—the hunt.

When we went to the air terminal to pick up a new hunter we always hoped we would see a strong individual with no fat on him, yet it was not always so. More often than not we would see a person who, although he might look like a very healthy person, would have a bit more weight than he needed. Since that was the case fairly often, we acted accordingly. We took the man on, took our time on the hunt, and got him up the mountain anyway. A guide must evaluate a hunter very well and learn all he can about the man before a hunt begins. Also the guide must pace himself to the speed the hunter can go, no matter if he is very slow getting up there. Obviously, the main thing for a guide to consider is that this man is paying a great deal of money for the hunt and the main objective is to get him the trophy desired. This fact must always be considered on each hunt.

Guides, who are almost always in good physical condition themselves, must take good care of their hunter. After a strenuous day of hunting, the guide—although he may be tired himself—must get the hunter back to the spike camp or base camp before dark—if possible. Then he must prepare a decent meal, letting the hunter rest while doing so.

Actually, some hunters improve as time goes on if the hunt is an extended one. With good rest periods, good food with a lot of calories, and strenuous exercise each day the hunter will soon get so he can go farther and faster each day. That result is always hoped for, but it does not always happen.

At any rate, remember that a sheep hunt is nothing like a deer or elk hunt. Get a program going several months before a hunt is to start and work hard on getting in good condition, even if it takes putting on a 25-pound pack and going up a small mountain as fast as possible. It will help a great deal and will make the actual hunt much more pleasurable.

I once had a repeat hunter who made it a point to be in absolutely great physical condition. All year around he exercised with the main objective being to get in superb condition for a hunt in the fall. Living in the Seattle area, he climbed mountains—which are easy to find in that country. In winter he spent a lot of time cross country skiing and just worked the year around to keep in good condition.

On his second hunt he wanted to get a record book ram—if possible—so we set out to get him one. In the Kotsina River drainage I had noticed a couple of old rams running together on a certain mountain system. One of them looked—from quite some distance—as if he would make the book. So we set out to get him—the hunter, whose name was Bill, and I, the guide.

We found the rams lying on a snow bank at about the 6,000 foot level. I thus had a chance to point out to Bill that sheep, although they appear to be pure white, are not actually so. A sheep lying on pure white snow will show that they are actually an off-white color with a slightly yellow tinge. I had noticed this many times during the winter months when the sheep are in snow country.

Sheep are slightly yellow and stand out against a snowy background— even in this b&w photo there is enough contrast to spot this ram.

We got up there where they lay on the snow and, since neither ram was looking our way, they did not see us and we spent quite a bit of time glassing them to figure out which was the best ram. Bill finally chose the ram on the left, shot it with one clean shot, and the ram died without even standing up. Then the other ram got up and trotted off the snowbank, stopped, and looked back at us. We could immediately see that he was the better ram of the two and most likely would have scored high enough to go in the book. Upon seeing this, Bill used some language I will not print here, and I don't blame him. Yet the shot had been made and there was absolutely nothing we could do about it. The ram Bill had taken was a very good one, however. The horns both measured an even 39 inches and were not broomed in any way. The bases were slightly less than 14 inches and it just would not point up big enough to make the book. It was most certainly a beautiful trophy, however, and Bill soon got over his consternation and was happy about it.

Getting back to being in good physical condition, I was to learn very soon that Bill was in much better condition than I was. I am a small, wiry man and during my active career could go up any mountain as rapidly as anyone. Yet I had never been any great shakes as a packer. The larger the man, the better packer he can be—it seems. I often employed a young, healthy man as a packer on these hunts; realizing it cost extra money, but it sometimes relieved me packing a heavy load off the mountain. This time I had not brought a packer, there was just Bill and I.

We carefully caped, skinned, and dressed the ram; then decided to take the entire carcass down to base camp rather than bone out the meat. We divided the load about equally between us, then started down the mountain.

Bill got in the lead and seemed to just stroll on down as if he was not packing anything at all. At the same time I was beginning to suffer and my knees felt as if they would break on the very next step. It may seem that it would be easy to go downhill with a heavy pack, but it is not so. Going down can be extremely hard on a person.

Bill, with his superb physical condition, got down to base camp quite some time before I made it. He was busying himself around camp, getting a fire going, and starting to prepare a meal before I even got there.

That is what really good physical condition can do for you. Try it before you come sheep hunting and it will be a much greater experience for you.

Preservation of Meat

The main objective of a sheep hunter is to get a trophy set of horns and usually a cape—so a nice head mount can be made by the hunter's chosen taxidermist. Beyond that, some hunters want no other part of the sheep.

Not only is a sheep one of the most striking and sought-after trophies, the meat is also exceptionally tasty.

There is the meat to consider, however; some of the best meat known—the wonderful meat of the wild sheep. If the hunter wants to have part of—or all of—the meat, there is no reason he should not have it in this modern day and age. It merely takes a bit of planning before the hunt begins; the hunter can easily arrange this with his outfitter or guide. Actually, once a hunter pulls the trigger and gets a sheep down, the entire animal becomes his property.

Often hunters bone out the meat to get rid of the bones, which are quite a bit of weight and worthless scraps as well. Also, there is generally some bloodshot meat that cannot be handled and must be left on the mountain. Sheep are always shot in the body, never the head or neck, so there is bound to be some bloodshot meat. Most of the meat will be good, however.

Rather than bone out the meat, a hunter might think of arranging so a young packer can go along on the hunt to help get the meat down off the mountain. Then butcher the carcass properly and take it all down. If you bone out the meat you will end up with merely a bag of meat, and not even a professional butcher can sort it out and make the proper cuts as desired for preparation of different dishes. There are plenty of professional butchers that cater to meat hunters in Alaska. If the entire carcass is taken to a good butcher he can make all the proper cuts, package it up the way the hunter desires, label each package, and have it ready for shipment.

During the August season it is still quite hot in Alaska. Yet the nights are getting cooler and it can sometimes even frost at night. So there is no real big rush about getting the meat butchered and frozen, although one must be aware that it is a good idea to get the meat taken care of within a few days.

Once the meat has been butchered up and packaged it can then be frozen; either by the butcher, if he has facilities for freezing the meat, or by the outfitter, who will have a deep freeze at his home. After meat has been frozen for two days it is as frozen as it will ever get and is ready to be shipped.

Most airlines will accommodate the hunter if he points out the box or boxes that have his frozen meat. They will see to it that the meat is placed in a cold baggage compartment. Since modern jets fly at very high, cold altitudes, you can be sure the meat will still be well frozen when you reach your destination in the Lower 48. After that it merely takes getting the meat into your own freezer; and there you will have it—delectable meat to enjoy and treat your family to.

photo courtesy of Jerry Lee©

The Time to go Hunting

Sheep season has, for years, opened on August 10 and remained open until September 20. This leaves a lengthy season for hunters to pick the proper time to go after one. Licenses can be bought right over the counter for most areas. There are certain management areas where permit hunting is in force and there are walk-in areas where aircraft or surface vehicles are banned, but most of Alaska is wide open for hunting.

A lot of hunters like to be out there on the mountain, ready to begin hunting on the morning the season opens. Therefore, for fly-in hunts there was quite a rush beginning on August eighth flying out the hunters to spots where there was access to good hunting. This early hunting has both advantages and disadvantages. It is true the sheep are settled down on their regular summer range and probably have not been disturbed all the year so they might be a bit easier to hunt successfully. Yet there are disadvantages, too. It gets too crowded and often more than one party will arrive at the same place at the same time. The first hunter that fires a rifle scares the sheep and off they go, away from there, across several mountains and into places where it is hard to hunt. Also there can be bad weather that will slow down hunts until it improves. Too many of the early hunters do not allot themselves the time needed for conducting a successful hunt and must go back to their job without having gotten a ram.

I liked to wait awhile until the big rush was over before beginning hunts, usually until August 20. By then, most of the early hunters were gone from the mountains and the sheep were settled down once more. It was generally better hunting if we waited until this later date.

In September the snow begins in the higher mountains, a harbinger of winter in a short time. The early snow in the high mountains is often an advantage. As the snow creeps lower on the mountain as the season progresses, the sheep move down with it and are easier to hunt. The disadvantage here is that a hunter may get snowed in and have to get out. It is not uncommon some years to snow as much as two feet, spoiling a hunt for certain.

So there is something to decide on—just when one wants to go hunting. Generally the period from about August twentieth until the tenth of September seems to be the best time to go—a quite lengthy period. The hunter who does not have any pressing duties elsewhere and can take a long time to get the hunting done will have the greatest success.

FACTS ABOUT SHEEP . . . 209

"The hunter who does not have any pressing duties elsewhere and can take a long time to get the hunting done will have the greatest success."

Jack Wilson (right) and and old friend, Fred Williams.

CHAPTER 19
THE LONG YEARS WENT BY

Great changes started taking place in the sheep hunting industry almost from the time of beginning for me, which was in the early 1950s. At the very first I practically had the south side of the Wrangells to myself. Hunting pressure was very light, especially in the eastern part where I began hunting each season. Right from the beginning I had started hunting north of the upper Chitina River, not far from the Yukon border of Canada. While I did not realize it at first, I had chosen the area of the Wrangell Mountains that had the largest concentration of exceptionaly large trophies. As time went on I was to find out this was actually fact: the country just naturally had sheep that were larger in body size and had long, flaring horns that went higher in the Boone and Crockett records than any other mountain system in Alaska. The exception was the number two Dall ram taken by Frank Cook in the Chugach Mountains in 1956. This ram became the number one record ram at that time. It held first place until Harry Swank took his new World Record ram in 1961 opposite, and north of, the Chitina Glacier; with me as the pilot and guide.

Yet there was extremely good sheep hunting in other parts of the Wrangells. There were many, many beautiful trophies out there roaming around that could be taken. Most of them just would not go as high in the book as those from the upper Chitina area, however. The spot on the Chetaslina drainage where Harley King and I built us a little airstrip opposite Sheep Gulch was one of these places. There were very many full curl rams for the taking and, at first, we could hunt in three directions from our new airstrip and expect to get good rams at any time we went hunting. We did not want to hunt that country too heavily since we had decided to crop our rams and not overdo it. Yet we did take quite a few over the next few years and had many happy, successful hunters.

Most of the hunters wanted a beautiful trophy for their expense and efforts, but did not necessarily feel they needed the largest record obtainable. These rams from the Sheep Gulch area would not point up high in the Book, yet they were beautiful rams and very few of them had broomed horns. They were ideal specimens.

We hunted in many of the drainages on the south side of the Wrangells and had good results; fine trophies, but not quite as large as those north of the upper Chitina river near the border. It was great hunting.

Most of the heavy hunting pressure was near the big population center in the Anchorage area. That portion of the Chugach Mountains and the Talkeetna Mountains were being heavily hunted in the 1950s, mostly because these mountains were closer and more accessible.

Aircraft of a certain type were what caused expansion to areas farther and farther from the big population centers. Since there were very few roads through any part of Alaska aircraft were by far the best means of transportation. There were many types of aircraft, but the Piper Super Cub won out. It was the very best light aircraft of all to conquer the tough places where there was no sign of an airstrip, but merely where a landing might be possible; someplace where good sheep hunting was offered. There were more of these light, extremely reliable machines being built every year by the Piper factory. And there were more pilots becoming adept at flying them each year and getting out there where the good sheep hunting was. Private pilots started getting Super Cubs and coming out to go hunting, following in the footsteps of those of us who considered ourselves professionals. Some of these pilots became very adept at flying and were sucessful hunters. Many of them, however, did not have all it took to be safe pilots and cracked up their airplanes.

"There were many types of aircraft, but the Piper Super Cub won out. It was the very best light aircraft of all to conquer the tough places where there was no sign of an airstrip, but merely where a landing might be possible; someplace where good sheep hunting was offered."

Each year there were several Cubs that cracked up out there. The pilot and his one passenger were not too often killed nor injured badly in these crackups, but sometimes they were killed at that. There have been Super Cubs getting damaged each year out there in the mountains for all these years and it is still happening to this day. Yet they keep coming. Super Cubs can always be rebuilt and fly once again, but the heavy cost is certainly something to be considered. There are many very good mechanics in Alaska that have good hangars and facilities merely for the purpose of rebuilding Super Cubs—making them once again as good as they were when the factory built them. All it takes is money and, depending on the amount of damage sustained, the amount can easily be determined.

The Biggest Sheep

It is interesting to note that many of the biggest sheep taken from Alaska came from my "bailiwick" above the upper Chitina River, or the great glaciers farther east—the Chitina and Logan Glaciers. Here was the Canadian border and it is possible that hunters sometimes got over the line and their sheep was actually killed in Canada. The border had been marked many years before with rock monuments, but they were quite far apart and not easily seen. But that is the area where many of the highest-scoring sheep came from.

According to their rank in the Boone and Crockett Records, 1971 edition, not only was the number one sheep taken in the upper Chitina River area, but also numbers 4,10,15,20 and 35. The number two sheep was taken by Frank Cook in the Chugach Mountains.

Those figures show that this area in Alaska was really unique in the amount of extremely large rams taken.

One old ram I saw closely one day when Dr. Frank Hibben took his large ram in 1963 above the Barnard Glacier was by far the biggest ram I had ever seen. I had a very good look at him after Frank killed his perfect ram which scored 178 in the book. This great ram was broomed on both horns, but they looked evenly broomed and those horns had the greatest mass of any sheep I had ever seen. The bases of those horns were noticeably tremendous and he might have been a new world record. In all my experience I had never seen a ram

James Harrower took this 181 3/8 pt. ram in Jack Wilson's baliwick in 1961.

with such massive horns.

I remembered that old ram and the next year sent a solo hunter after him. This hunter packed up the mountain and spent a long time trying to find him—with no luck.

Apparently we were too late and the old ram was dead. He spent quite a bit of time looking for the carcass and horns, but again, with no luck. I had shown the old ram to Harry Swank before he killed the World Record farther up the river. We had a good look at him from the air—at a distance so he would not be disturbed—and we used our field glasses to observe him. For this flight we were using a Cessna 185, slowed down as much as possible. It was a pretty good aircraft for observing things below and beyond us. Harry had a desire to go after the old boy, yet there seemed to be some drawbacks. From the air we could see that he was broomed on both horns and we named him "Old Broomie." We could tell his horns had great bases, but of course we could not count the age rings on the horns from the air. Harry decided to go after the old ram up above Ram Glacier, did so, and got him—as related in another chapter. I have always wondered if "Old Broomie" might have scored even higher in the book than the one he had taken . . .

I was personally acquainted with all those hunters who got the biggest record book sheep in the upper Chitina area. All of them, with the exception of Frank Hibben, used their own airplanes. I was Hibben's guide when we took his perfect ten-year-old ram above Barnard Glacier. I skinned out the entire ram for a full mount. As far as I know that ram is mounted at the University of Albuquerque Museum. At least that was where it was supposed to go.

Hunters moved out further and further into the Wrangells as time went by until they were coming hot and heavy—even as far as the eastern Wrangells. More guides showed up every year and more private hunters as well. It became necessary to be secretive about where we hunted and not mention the places we landed to begin a sheep hunt. I landed in places out near mountains, or upon the mountain itself, and moved in the hunters. Then when the hunt was completed, we obliterated all sign that we had ever been there. We left nothing that could be seen by an alert pilot that showed we had ever used the spot for a landing followed by a hunt. We left not even a candy wrapper to show our presence there. While using a secret strip we erected runway markers using paper plates stood on edge, and if there was brush there we hung streamers on it to indicate wind direction. But when we left we were careful to remove all of these things to keep snoopy pilots from finding out where we had begun a hunt.

By far the greatest change in the sheep hunting was because of the creation of several very large National Parks. For years there had been debate about creating new parks in Alaska and the movement grew greater each year. Alaska is mostly Federal land and Alaskans themselves had very little to say about what was to be done with their great state. It seemed that certain groups, and also the Federal Government, wanted to set aside much more land than was needed for these new parks. Alaskans had very little to say about what would be done.

Our past President, Jimmy Carter, set aside many millions of acres in Alaska as National Monuments before he left office. It was then up to Congress to act upon this within a reasonable time.

We were afraid that all hunting would be stopped within the new parks and that would have been a terrible blow to hunters. However, we were to learn that at least part of every new park would be preserves where hunting would still be allowed.

Congress finalized the Alaska National Parks and Preserves on December 2, 1980 and we had to learn about them and take note of the great changes it would make to us as hunters and guides. There are now many National Parks, Preserves, Monuments, Historical Parks, and so on within the State.

Jack's baliwick—the upper Chitna River—is now part of Wrangell-St. Elias National Park and Preserve; currently visited by only a few subsistence hunters each year.

The biggest National Park within the United States was the one that involved those of us who lived and worked in the Copper River Basin, the new Wrangell-St. Elias National Park. With the Copper River as the southwest boundary for a good bit of it the park encompassed 13.2 million acres, but one million is either state, Native, or private lands. A good bit of it is in the park preserve where hunting is allowed. This is still more or less regulated by the state, but most of it is within the park boundary which is federally regulated. That means, for reasons unknown to any of us, certain good areas for trophy sheep were in the park and could not be hunted. Most of my old guide area was taken in the park, leaving me no place to hunt. From the Canadian border clear west almost to the Barnard Glacier—where there was such good hunting and where the biggest trophies of all were taken—was now within the park where nothing but subsistence hunting was allowed.

The Wrangell-St. Elias became the largest National Park in the United States. It took in all the Wrangell Mountains, all the St. Elias Mountains within Alaska, and a big part of the Chugach Mountains to the south. Combined with the Kluane National Park and Preserve across the border in Canada, the two parks became the largest National Park in the world.

Mineral exploration in the new Wrangell-St. Elias Park and Preserve came to a halt. Some of the largest mining companies in the world had, for many years, conducted this exploration. At least there would no longer be helicopters scaring "my" sheep. All the information the mining companies had gotten about mineral deposits in the Wrangells would forever be locked away in their files. They had spent millions for their information—never to be disclosed to the public.

Subsistence hunting by a very few Alaska residents is still allowed within the parks, but access is the problem. Aircraft are not allowed to transport hunters into the National Park where subsistence hunting—but not trophy hunting—is allowed. Even if a subsistence hunter actually desires a big trophy, there are too many obstacles in the way. As far as hunting in my old area up at the headwaters of the Chitina River and into the great glaciers—it is nearly impossible to get there. It is legal to use a riverboat for access, but the Chitina River is a glacial, muddy, braided stream. It is impossible to tell how deep the water is and river boats have a lot of trouble going aground when trying to negotiate the small streams, so it does not work very well.

So the great trophy rams are out there and always will be. Only the extremely hardy will ever even see or photograph them. The ordinary person does not stand a chance of getting way out there and seeing them at all.

But do not let that deter you. There are still many millions of acres of land in our great state to hunt sheep where it is allowed and accessible. It is not necessary to hunt within the National Parks. There are many, many places to go in quest of a good, trophy ram.

So go a-hunting. Choose a place where there are many sheep and where access is allowed and go on. Have a great, enjoyable experience and take plenty of time for a good hunt. Under the full curl law there are rams growing up to fit that status every year. And who knows? Perhaps you will run into that old boy that has eluded hunters for years, the greatest trophy of all, and he will come under your sights. Even if your dreams in that respect do not come true, you can still get a beautiful trophy to put on your wall. Hunting pressure has been heavy ever since World War II came to an end, yet it has never gotten so heavy that there is not a possibility to take a fine trophy Dall ram. It is just a bit more difficult nowadays and takes a bit more time. Perseverance and good stamina is what it takes.

Go, and enjoy . . .

TONY RUSS
REGISTERED ALASKAN GUIDE

SPECIALIZING IN:
TROPHY DALL SHEEP HUNTS IN THE TALKEETNA AND CHUGACH MOUNTAINS

As of 2000, Tony has taken five Pope & Young Record Book Dall sheep with bow & arrow–including the P&Y **WORLD RECORD DALL SHEEP.** All hunters will hunt personally with Tony – no assistant guides. Call or write for more information: Tony Russ, 574 Sarahs Way, Wasilla, AK, 99654; 907-376-6474.

Kyle Meintzer with 2000 ram taken with guide Tony Russ

ORDER FORM

THE QUEST FOR DALL SHEEP: A Historic Guide's Memories of Alaskan Hunting, by Jack Wilson, 224 pages, 90 photos, $19.95..............$_____

SHEEP HUNTING IN ALASKA: The Dall Sheep Hunter's Guide, by Tony Russ, 160 pages, 57 photos, $19.95......................................$_____

THE MANUAL FOR SUCCESSFUL HUNTERS: Why 10% of the Hunters Take 90% of the Game, by Tony Russ, 400 pages, 170 photos, 40 illustrations, $24.95...$_____

BOWHUNTING ALASKA, a how-to guide by Ron Swanson, updated in 1997 by Tony Russ, 62 pages, 33 photos, 10 maps, $10.00........................$_____

ALASKA BOWHUNTING RECORDS: Bowhunting records of Alaska's big game animals, by Tony Russ, 128 pages, 23 photos, HARDCOVER; $25.00...........$_____

BOOK TOTAL.........................$_____

SHIPPING ($3 for first book, $1 each add'l book).........$_____

TOTAL ENCLOSED (check or money order made out to Northern Publishing)......$_____

Send books to: _____

_____

_____

Mail Order Form to: Northern Publishing
                      574 Sarahs Way
                      Wasilla, AK 99654

HORN & ANTLER CARVINGS
by TONY RUSS

Native Alaskan, guide, writer, and bowhunter.

Creations that depict the beauty and majesty of Alaska and her wildlife, captured in materials from the animals themselves.

(Contact Tony at address/phone number on previous page.)

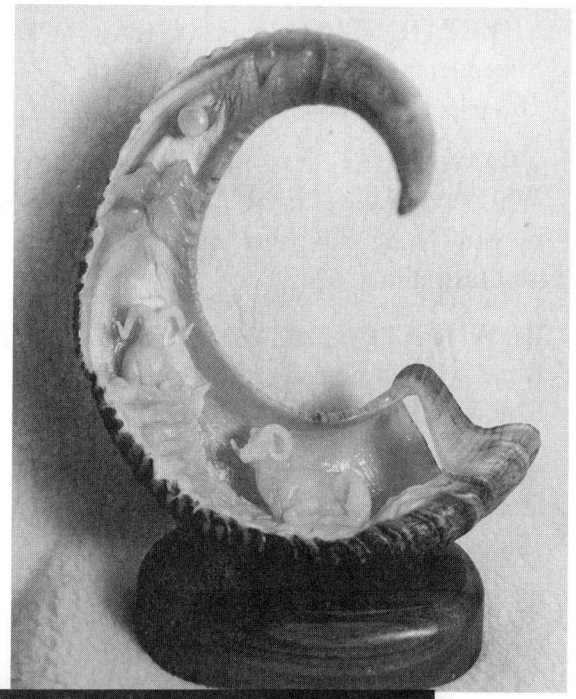

Moose, Caribou, and sheep horn carvings from your design or mine.